JOHN FLOWER
with additional material by Vicki Lywood Last

FIRST CERTIFICATE ORGANISER

New Syllabus Edition

Д. Флауэр

Сборник упражнений для подготовки
к вступительному экзамену по английскому языку
в университеты Англии (с ключами)
(Для тех, кто хочет знать уровень своей языковой подготовки)

Обнинск · Издательство "Титул" · 1997

ББК 81.2–922(923) Англ
Ф70

Language Teaching Publications

35 Church Road, Hove, BN3 2BE, England

NO UNAUTHORISED PHOTOCOPYING

The Author

John Flower is a teacher at Eurocentre Bournemouth where he has worked for many years. He has long experience of teaching students at all levels, and has always had a keen interest in preparing students for the Cambridge examinations. He is the author of the *Build Your Vocabulary* series and *Phrasal Verb Organiser*.

Acknowledgements

We are grateful to all the many teachers, schools and students who commented upon this material while in development.

We are most grateful to Vicki Lywood Last, who brought her long experience of examining for the Cambridge First Certificate examinations to this book. Her help was particularly useful in the Revision Grammar, Common Mistakes, and Examination Preparation sections.

The author would like to thank Michael Lewis and Jimmie Hill for all their help and guidance, and Ruth, Andrew, and Helen for putting up with it all.

Cover Design by Anna Macleod
Printed in England by Commercial Colour Press, London E7

Flower J. **First Certificate Organiser**.— Флауэр Д. **Сборник упражнений для подготовки к**
Ф70 **вступительному экзамену по английскому языку в университеты Англии (с ключа-ми)**.— Обнинск: Титул, 1997. 208 с.

ISBN 5-86866-080-3

    "Сборник упражнений для подготовки к вступительному экзамену по английскому языку в университеты Англии" Джона Флауэра издается в России по лицензии английского издательства LTP. Это учебное пособие охватывает все аспекты английского языка, которые контролируются на вступительном экзамене: грамматику, лексику, темы для устного высказывания, анализируются типичные ошибки и т. д. Все упражнения снабжены ключами.

    Для учащихся старших классов и студентов 1—2 курсов вузов.

ББК 81.2–922(923) Англ

To the Student . . . .

BEFORE YOU START

This book will help you to organise the language **you** need for the Cambridge First Certificate.

Most units have a double page. On the left-hand page there is an exercise which introduces and practises important language.

The right-hand page **organises** the language so that you can learn it more effectively.

On this page you will also find some extra examples.

You are encouraged to extend your vocabulary by adding more items to the lists.

Just before the exam you can use the right-hand pages to help you **revise** quickly and easily. Cover over the lists you have made and check that you can remember.

There are several things you can do to learn English in an effective and efficient way.

- Work regularly. Try to do one or two units every day.

- Do different types of exercises. If you do two units at one time, choose them from different sections of the book.

- Don't learn a word in isolation. Learn it with other words that often occur with it.

- Personalise your learning. Make your own examples using the words and expressions you have studied in the book. Try to write true things that you might want to use in the examination.

- Make a habit of reading and listening to English. The more you do this, the more natural your English will become.

- As you find new vocabulary, note it down in a systematic way. For guidance, look at the way the language is organised in this book.

- The more organised your learning is, the better you will do in the examination.

Contents

Contents

WORD PARTNERSHIPS *1*

As you study the vocabulary you need for the First Certificate, you will soon realise that it is not enough to study single words. It is important to know how words combine with others to form partnerships. This will help you to produce language of the level required to do well in the examination.

Take the word 'fun' as an example. Look at these two sentences:
> Did you have fun at the party last night?
> I wish he wouldn't make fun of my accent.

From these two sentences you should learn the expressions:
> **have fun** and **make fun of**

and write sentences of your own to help you to remember them.

Word partnerships are important in every part of the examination, but your knowledge of them is specially tested in Paper 3 (Use of English).

In two exercises you have to use one word to fill in a blank, for example:

> Jimmy made his way to the station exit. This was the first time he had been to London
> (10) .... his own and he was feeling a bit scared.

In one exercise you have to think of the word yourself, and in the other you are given a choice:
> 10.　　A by　　B for　　C on　　D in

The answer is **C** because the expression is **on his own**.

As you read through that extract, did you notice another useful word partnership, **made his way?**

Word partnerships are also important in the exercise in which you complete a sentence so that it means the same as the first sentence you are given, for example:

There must always be somebody with her.
own
She should not be left .... at any time.

Being **aware of** these partnerships will enable you to **build up your vocabulary** so that you can use it when you **take your exam**.

Word Partnerships . . . . INTRODUCTION

In this book you will find many examples of word partnerships but it is essential that you try to find your own words.

Look at the following news item. How many useful word partnerships can you find?

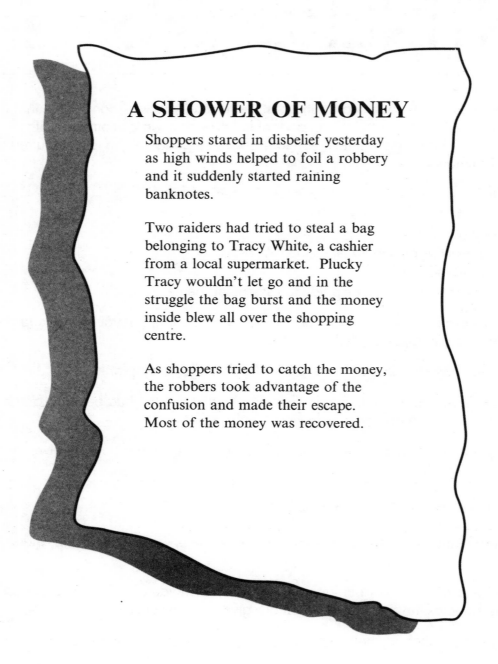

A SHOWER OF MONEY

Shoppers stared in disbelief yesterday as high winds helped to foil a robbery and it suddenly started raining banknotes.

Two raiders had tried to steal a bag belonging to Tracy White, a cashier from a local supermarket. Plucky Tracy wouldn't let go and in the struggle the bag burst and the money inside blew all over the shopping centre.

As shoppers tried to catch the money, the robbers took advantage of the confusion and made their escape. Most of the money was recovered.

Now organise the partnerships you have found by doing the exercise on the opposite page.

Word Partnerships . . . . INTRODUCTION

From the passage you have just read, write down one example of:

a noun and verb partnership   ....

a verb and noun partnership   ....

an adjective and noun   ....

a verb and preposition   ....

a preposition and noun   ....

a verb, noun and preposition   ....

Look at the bottom of the page for some suggested partnerships.

In this book you will usually find an exercise on the right-hand page in which you have to organise vocabulary to make it easier to learn for the examination. You will often be asked to provide your own examples to add to the lists.

You will see how important it is to collect words not individually, but in groups which often occur together. This is the kind of thing you should be doing every time you read or listen to English. It is one of the best ways to make significant progress in your ability to use the language!

noun + verb: *the bag burst*
verb + noun: *foil a robbery, made their escape*
adjective + noun: *high winds, local supermarket*
verb + preposition: *belonging to*
preposition + noun: *in disbelief, in the struggle*
verb, noun + preposition: *took advantage of*

1.1 Adjective + Preposition – 1 . . . .

Complete each sentence by using an adjective from the list on the left and a preposition from the list on the right.
You must use each adjective once only but you can use each preposition more than once.

accustomed	dependent	proud		at
afraid	famous	ready		for
ashamed	full	relevant		of
aware	good	responsible		on
capable	jealous	typical		to

1. She was .... her friend because she had a better dress.

2. The waste paper bin was .... crumpled sheets of paper.

3. This computer is .... producing sophisticated graphics.

4. The town is especially .... its elegant architecture.

5. I felt very .... making such a stupid mistake.

6. After weeks of preparation the hall is nearly .... the grand opening.

7. Could you add this up for me? I'm not very .... maths.

8. Who is .... writing those words on the wall?

9. She was so .... her nephew's achievement that she couldn't stop talking about it.

10. It took some time to get .... the pace of life in the country after the frantic atmosphere of the town.

11. We try to eat food which is .... the region in which we are travelling.

12. Are you .... any reason why he should be late?

13. They built nuclear power stations so as not to be .... coal as their main source of energy.

14. This is not really .... our discussion so can we get back to the main point of the meeting?

15. He sleeps with the light on because he's .... the dark.

Complete each group of partnerships with the correct preposition.

1. accustomed .... peace and quiet
    getting up late
    so much noise

9. good .... her job
    adding up
    English

2. afraid .... the dark
    making a mistake
    saying something silly

10. jealous .... what other people do
    her rich friends
    his English!

3. ashamed .... yourself
    what I've done
    doing a thing like that

4. aware .... a strange smell
    people staring
    looking rather untidy

11. proud .... her grandson
    his work
    what he's done

5. capable .... high speeds
    working fast
    anything!

12. ready .... anything
    bed
    the next question

6. dependent .... imports
    how he feels
    what happens

13. relevant .... the argument
    our discussion
    the problem

7. famous .... its museums
    making pottery
    his paintings

14. responsible .... the equipment
    making a mess
    France and Italy

8. full .... pride
    fun
    dark green liquid

15. typical .... the region
    the way he acts
    people who ....

Test yourself from time to time by covering the words that follow each adjective. How many partnership words can you remember?

1.2 Adjective + Preposition – 2 . . . .

Complete each sentence by using an adjective from the list on the left and a preposition from the list on the right.
You must use each adjective once only but you can use each preposition more than once.

absent	opposed	suitable		at	for
better	satisfied	suspicious		from	of
guilty	short	terrified		on	to
keen	similar	terrible		with	
late	sorry	tired			

1. Because of the flu epidemic many staff were .... work.

2. They were .... strangers so they kept following us around and watching what we were doing.

3. I feel really .... her because she has to do all the work while the others go out and enjoy themselves.

4. They won't be .... just a small party! They'll want to invite every single one of their friends!

5. I must hurry or I'll be .... work.

6. She's never been very .... going to meetings so I wouldn't be surprised if she doesn't turn up.

7. The jury found him .... robbing the bank.

8. We're totally .... the road-widening scheme and will fight it all the way.

9. She's much .... driving than he is.

10. I'm a bit .... money at the moment so could you pay?

11. She's not really .... this job. We wanted someone older.

12. This incident is very .... what happened yesterday except that it was later on in the day.

13. She wouldn't tell her father because she was .... what he might do if he lost his temper.

14. I can recognise faces but I'm .... remembering names!

15. He got .... hearing the same old excuses, day after day.

Complete each group of partnerships with the correct preposition.

1. absent .... school
work
the meeting

2. better .... sport than me
explaining things
maths

3. guilty .... wasting time
murder
not listening

4. keen .... football
making models
fashion

5. late .... the meeting
work
school

6. opposed .... this scheme
paying so much
wasting more money

7. satisfied .... the result
what I've done
how things went

8. short .... money
breath
time

9. similar .... my dress
what I saw
the one I've got

10. sorry .... yourself
what I said
being late

11. suitable .... handicapped people
children
the time of year

12. suspicious .... strangers
everything he says
people who ask
questions

13. terrified .... missing the train
what he'll do
being alone

14. terrible .... mathematics
spelling
remembering names

15. tired .... this weather
eating this stuff
waiting

Test yourself from time to time by covering the words that follow each adjective. How many partnership words can you remember?

1.3 **Verb + Preposition – 1** . . . .

Complete each sentence with the correct form of one of the verbs below and the
preposition **from** or **on**.
Use each verb once only.

borrow	decide	escape	prevent	resign
concentrate	depend	insist	recover	retire
congratulate	differ	operate	rely	suffer

1. She .... her job after she was offered another with more
   responsibility and a higher salary.

2. He might come. It will .... how he feels.

3. You must .... the road when you're driving!

4. He got very annoyed and .... seeing the manager.

5. The surgeon .... her immediately and saved her life.

6. I decided to .... my job early even though it meant I wouldn't
   get such a good pension.

7. It will take her weeks to .... such a major operation so she won't
   be back at work for some time.

8. We had security men on the door to .... unwanted guests .... getting
   into the party.

9. I've sent her a card to .... her .... passing her test.

10. The bank wouldn't lend me the money so I had to .... it .... my
    parents.

11. This design .... slightly .... the first one I showed you.

12. I .... backache so I have to go to a physiotherapist once a week.

13. After weeks of discussion they've finally .... the new colour
    scheme for the staff canteen.

14. They managed to .... the prison by bribing a guard.

15. You can .... Frances to keep you up to date with all the latest
    gossip.

Now put the correct preposition in each group of partnerships.

1. **borrow a book** .... the library
   my parents
   a friend of his

9. **operate** .... a patient

2. **concentrate** .... your work
   driving
   what I'm doing

10. **prevent** .... doing what they want
    leaving
    cheating

3. **congratulate** .... his results
   her success
   winning

11. **recover** .... a cold
    a serious illness
    a nasty shock

4. **decide** .... a colour scheme
   which to choose
   the (blue) one

12. **rely** .... every employee
    you to do your best
    the bus service

5. **depend** .... imports
   how I feel
   if I have time or not

13. **resign** .... the committee
    his job

6. **differ** .... the others
   what I expected
   what I really wanted

14. **retire** .... work at 65

7. **escape** .... prison
   this routine
   the crowd

8. **insist** .... good service
   seeing **her**
   punctuality

15. **suffer** .... a headache
    toothache
    a bad cold

Notice when you need an ...**ing** form of the verb. This is important in the exam.

1.4 **Verb + Preposition – 2** . . . .

Complete each sentence with the correct form of one of the verbs below and the preposition **of**, **for**, **in** or **to**.
Use each verb once only.

accuse	believe	consist	object	search
apologise	belong	forgive	pay	specialise
approve	blame	hope	remind	succeed

1. The test .... two written papers and an interview.

2. I've kept the luggage label as a souvenir to .... me .... the wonderful holiday we had.

3. After taking a general course she decided to .... tropical medicine.

4. After trying for an hour I finally .... starting the car.

5. Where will I find the money to .... a new suit?

6. That coat .... Andrew and this is Ricky's.

7. Some guests have .... having to pay extra to use the swimming pool. I'm not surprised they're annoyed!

8. Army helicopters were brought in to help .... the missing children.

9. I had never .... ghosts until I stayed at a mysterious old house in the country.

10. He wrote a letter .... all the trouble he had caused and asking her to forgive him.

11. He's the person in charge. I .... him .... the mix-up.

12. By the way she spoke you could see that she didn't .... the arrangements for the wedding.

13. I don't think I'll ever .... her .... the way she made me look such a fool in front of all those people.

14. The policeman .... him .... breaking into the house but he said he could prove he had been somewhere else.

15. Let's .... the best. You never know – the weather might clear up.

Now put the correct preposition in each group of partnerships.
Pay careful attention to the expressions which are followed by the ... **ing** form of the verb.

1. accuse 🧍 .... murder
breaking **in**
not **car**ing

2. apologise .... my mistake
being **late**
forgetting

3. approve .... all-night TV
his friends
smoking

4. believe .... healthy exercise
eating well
ghosts

5. belong .... my dog
a friend of mine
everyone

6. blame 🧍 .... the disaster
what happenened
getting angry

7. consist .... two parts
three sections
five papers

8. forgive 🧍 .... what he did
leaving me
not **asking**

9. hope .... the best
a good result
better luck next time!

10. object .... the by-pass
paying extra
🧍 **us**ing my phone

11. pay .... the meal
having my car fixed
wasting so much time

12. remind 🧍 .... my holiday
the time we ....
something that
happened to me....

13. search .... the solution
the missing children
somewhere to stay

14. specialise .... fast food
commercial French
selling furniture

15. succeed .... my attempts to ...
meeting her
passing my exam

1.5 **Verb + Noun + Preposition – 1** . . . .

In this exercise you must complete each sentence with a suitable verb and preposition from the lists below.
You may use each verb or preposition more than once.
Make sure you use the correct form of the verb!

---

catch	keep	lose	take		of	on	to
make	pay	put					

---

1. She .... advantage .... her father's good mood and asked if her boyfriend could stay for dinner.

2. Was anybody .... attention .... what she was saying?

3. Could you .... care .... our dog while we're on holiday?

4. She .... charge .... the project when Mr East was away.

5. I've .... count .... the number of times he's said that.

6. Could you .... an eye .... the washing while I'm out?

7. I wish she wouldn't .... such a fuss .... her nephew! You can see he really hates it!

8. .... no notice .... him! He's just showing off!

9. The salesman started to .... pressure .... her to sign the agreement straightaway.

10. While I was watching the match, I .... sight .... them standing at the back of the crowd.

11. We must .... a stop .... all this arguing.

12. Don't forget you'll have to .... tax .... that money you earned, so you're not as rich as you thought you were!

| **STUDY TIP** | Look back at the exercise and underline the complete word partnership in each sentence (for example, *catch sight of someone.*) |

Complete the first column by using the partnerships from the exercise and these four expressions.

set fire ....   **make sense ....**   **take pity ....**   **play a trick ....**

Space has been left for you to add your own partnerships.

PHRASE		MEANING
1.	of	benefit while you can
2.	of	look after
3.	of	be in control
4.	of	not remember how many
5.	of	hug, kiss, give presents etc.
6.	of	ignore
7.	of	understand
8.	of	see suddenly
9.	on	watch, check now and again
10.	on	feel very sorry for
11.	on	try to persuade
12.	on	give money to the government!
13.	on	deceive
14.	to	listen carefully
15.	to	start something burning
16.	to	not allow to continue
....		....
....		....
....		....
....		....
....		....
....		....

Test yourself later by covering the first column and looking at the definition on the right.

2*

1.6 **Verb + Noun + Preposition – 2** . . . .

Complete each sentence with the correct form of **make** or **take** and one of the prepositions below.
You may use each preposition more than once.

| **for** | **from** | **in** | **off** | **with** |

---

1. He's very shy so it's not easy to .... friends .... him.

2. I've still got to .... all the arrangements .... the party next weekend.

3. He refused to .... all the credit .... the success and said that it had been a team effort.

4. Many local people have .... an active interest .... our plans to bring live music back to the town.

5. For the first few months he .... great pride .... showing people around his new house.

6. I watched a comedy programme to try and .... my mind .... what had happened.

7. Why should I .... the blame .... the mix-up?

8. We've moved the wardrobe to .... room .... an extra bed.

9. We don't .... a charge .... repairs if the item is still under guarantee.

10. She's agreed to .... part .... next month's show.

11. I finally .... contact .... him at his New York office.

12. She's .... a remarkable recovery .... her illness.

Underline the complete word partnership in each sentence above.

| **STUDY TIP** | There are a lot of word partnerships that include the verbs **make** and **take**. This means that there could be a question in Paper 3 (Use of English) with an expression using either of these two words. |

Below you will see a list of word partnerships with **make** and **take**.
Most are from the exercise opposite but some more have been added.
Supply the missing preposition in each case.
Space has been left for you to add any more partnerships that you find.

1. **You make an application** .... a job as a secretary.

2. **You make arrangements** .... the party next week.

3. **You make a charge** .... repairing the broken door.

4. **You make contact** .... a customer by telex.

5. **You make friends** .... other members of the class.

6. **You make a recovery** .... a serious illness.

7. **You make room** .... an extra person at table.

8. **You take the blame** .... what went wrong.

9. **You take the credit** .... making the party a success.

10. **You take an interest** .... the project.

11. **You take a look** .... some important papers.

12. **You take your mind** .... what happened.

13. **You take part** .... a competition.

14. **You take great pleasure** .... presenting her with her prize.

15. **You take pride** .... showing the model you've made.

....

....

....

....

....

....

....

1.7 **Noun + Verb** . . . .

Match each noun on the left with a verb on the right. Use each word once only. Write your answers in the boxes.

EXERCISE 1

1. an accident	**a.** barks		1	
2. a dog	**b.** beats		2	
3. a heart	**c.** boils		3	
4. snow	**d.** falls		4	
5. the sun	**e.** fits		5	
6. a sweater	**f.** happens		6	
7. a team	**g.** loses		7	
8. a telephone	**h.** passes		8	
9. time	**i.** rings		9	
10. water	**j.** shines		10	

EXERCISE 2   Now do the same with these words.

1. a band	**a.** burns		1	
2. a car	**b.** fades		2	
3. a carton of milk	**c.** gathers		3	
4. a colour	**d.** itches		4	
5. a crowd	**e.** lands		5	
6. a fire	**f.** leaks		6	
7. a nose	**g.** plays		7	
8. a patient	**h.** recovers		8	
9. a plane	**i.** sails		9	
10. a ship	**j.** skids		10	

Now write sentences using the partnerships you have seen.
Can you think of any more verbs that can follow the nouns above?

Put each of the following nouns once only in a suitable partnership.
Put another verb with each noun. (For help, look at the opposite page.)

a band	a crowd	a heart	a ship	a sweater
a car	a dog	a nose	snow	a team
a colour	a fire	a plane	the sun	water

1. .... rises
sets
....

9. .... crashes
starts
....

2. .... grows
cheers
....

10. .... practises
wins
....

3. .... drifts
melts
....

11. .... freezes
flows
....

4. .... floats
sinks
....

5. .... crashes
flies
....

12. .... growls
bites
....

6. .... pounds
breaks!
....

13. .... performs
rehearses
....

7. .... stretches
shrinks
....

14. .... clashes
matches
....

8. .... spreads
glows
....

15. .... bleeds
runs
....

1.8 **Verb + Noun** . . . .

Match each verb on the left with a noun on the right. Some verbs can be followed by more than one noun but you must use each word once only. Write your answers in the boxes.

EXERCISE 1

1.	catch	**a.**	breakfast		1	
2.	change	**b.**	your breath		2	
3.	do	**c.**	your own business		3	
4.	give	**d.**	a corner		4	
5.	have	**e.**	(me) a favour		5	
6.	hold	**f.**	fire		6	
7.	mind	**g.**	house		7	
8.	move	**h.**	your mind		8	
9.	take	**i.**	permission		9	
10.	turn	**j.**	place		10	

EXERCISE 2 Now do the same with these words.

1.	do	**a.**	evidence		1	
2.	give	**b.**	an example		2	
3.	have	**c.**	fun		3	
4.	keep	**d.**	home		4	
5.	lead	**e.**	a mistake		5	
6.	leave	**f.**	a seat		6	
7.	make	**g.**	the truth		7	
8.	set	**h.**	the washing-up		8	
9.	take	**i.**	watch		9	
10.	tell	**j.**	the way		10	

Now write sentences using the partnerships you have found.

Put each of the following verbs once only in a suitable partnership. Put another noun with each verb. (For help, look at the opposite page.)

catch	change	do	give	have	hold	keep
leave	make	set	take	tell	turn	

1. .... the page
the handle
....

8. .... a bus
a cold
....

2. .... a meeting
my hand
....

9. .... your homework
the ironing
....

3. .... your time
her temperature
....

10. .... lies
a story
....

4. .... a message
a space
....

5. .... advice
an interview
....

11. .... a light bulb
trains
....

6. .... a headache
a shower
....

12. .... a secret
a diary
....

7. .... progress
a noise
....

13. .... some homework
the alarm
....

STUDY TIP The four verbs **give, have, make** and **take** form many partnerships so it is worth noting down any new expressions you meet.
Write a sentence for each of the expressions.
This will help you to remember what they mean and how they are used.

1.9 **Verb + Noun (Antonyms)** . . . .

In this exercise you will see sentences which include a verb in capital letters. You have to fill each blank with the antonym (opposite) of that verb.
Choose from the list of verbs below. Use each verb once only and make sure you use the correct form of the verb.

accept	fail	keep	nod
attack	forget	lengthen	tighten
catch	hide	lower	
deny	hit	miss	

1. He refused to CONFIRM or .... the report.

2. I .... the bus this morning so I'll get there early tomorrow to make sure I CATCH it.

3. He .... his head if he agreed and SHOOK his head if he didn't.

4. They've RAISED a few prices and .... some others.

5. Do you really expect her to .... her promise after she's BROKEN so many others?

6. He was the only one who .... my offer after all the others had REJECTED it.

7. I'll THROW the ball and you can .... it.

8. Only one bullet .... the target. All the others MISSED.

9. I can REMEMBER where it was I met her but I've .... when.

10. Rather than .... the lunch break, they want to SHORTEN it.

11. The first time I took my driving test, I .... In fact, I only PASSED at the fourth attempt.

12. We were supposed to .... our feelings and not SHOW any emotion, whatever happened.

13. He thought he was .... the mechanism but in fact he was LOOSENING it.

14. Their forwards were .... the goal so almost the whole team raced back to DEFEND it.

Put an antonym in each blank. Use these for the new partnerships:

borrow   **complicate**   **enter**   **lose**   **save**   **strengthen**

Space has been left for you to add more examples of your own.

1. accept .... an offer

2. attack .... a proposal

3. break .... a promise

4. catch .... a bus

5. confirm .... a statement

6. fail .... a test

7. gain .... confidence

8. lend .... money

9. leave .... a building

10. miss .... the target

11. nod .... your head

12. raise .... prices

13. remember .... a name

14. show .... your feelings

15. shorten .... a skirt

16. simplify .... matters

17. throw .... a ball

18. tighten .... your grip

19. waste .... time

20. weaken .... an argument

....

....

....

....

1.10 Adjective + Noun (Antonyms) . . . .

Complete each sentence by using an adjective which is opposite in meaning to the adjective in capital letters.
Use an adjective from the list below.
Use each adjective once only.

artificial	emotional	light	stale
busy	exact	low	superior
calm	flexible	rapid	
dark	gentle	shallow	

1. The scarf looked black in .... light but here, in NATURAL light, I can see it's really dark blue.

2. I started swimming at the .... end but I soon felt brave enough to go to the DEEP end.

3. I want the .... figures, not APPROXIMATE ones!

4. Most days are QUIET but some can be very ....

5. When we sailed, the sea was .... but it soon got very ROUGH.

6. He gave me a .... smile, which made me feel very INFERIOR.

7. I always eat a .... lunch because my keep-fit teacher says that HEAVY meals are bad for you.

8. He got very .... when he heard the news, but she stayed CALM.

9. We'll go swimming when it's .... tide. The beach is completely covered at HIGH tide.

10. Why does he have such a RIGID attitude? If he were more ...., I'm sure we could come to some kind of agreement.

11. The bread in this country goes .... very quickly so we buy it FRESH every day.

12. At first, progress was .... but later it became very SLOW as we met some unforeseen difficulties.

13. What had started out as a .... breeze soon became a very STRONG wind.

14. One daughter had .... hair while the other had FAIR hair.

Put an antonym in each blank. Use these words for the new partnerships:

considerable   **mild**   **poor**   **severe**   **smooth**   **worthless**

Space has been left for you to add more examples of your own.

1. **artificial**   ....   **light**
2. **calm**   ....   **sea**
3. **calm**   ....   **response**
4. **dark**   ....   **skin**
5. **deep**   ....   **water**
6. **exact**   ....   **time**
7. **flexible**   ....   **policy**
8. **good**   ....   **health**
9. **high**   ....   **opinion**
10. **light**   ....   **meal**
11. **mild**   ....   **winter**
12. **quiet**   ....   **day**
13. **rapid**   ....   **progress**
14. **rough**   ....   **surface**
15. **slight**   ....   **change**
16. **stale**   ....   **food**
17. **strong**   ....   **taste**
18. **strong**   ....   **wind**
19. **superior**   ....   **quality**
20. **valuable**   ....   **painting**

....

....

....

....

1.11 **Phrases** with **In** . . . .

Complete each sentence with one of the phrases from the list below.
Use each phrase once only.

in common	**in a moment**	**in public**
in the end	**in pain**	**in silence**
in ink	**in the past**	**in tears**
in love	**in pieces**	**in time**

1. I found her .... after her boyfriend had walked out on her, so I tried to cheer her up.

2. He wasn't too happy at first but .... we managed to persuade him.

3. In the exam you must write your answers ...., not pencil, otherwise you'll be **in trouble!**

4. The dog was obviously .... so the vet gave him an injection **in order to** stop it hurting so much.

5. They listened to him .... and even after he'd finished, it was some time before anyone spoke.

6. .... families used to stay together but nowadays they often live in different parts of the country.

7. If we hurry we might get to the station ....

8. She looks confident but **in fact** she's never sung .... before today.

9. They have so little .... but **in spite of** this he's still going out with her.

10. **In addition to** the mirror, I found a vase lying .... on the floor.

11. He should be back .... so would you like to sit down and wait for him?

12. You could tell they were .... by the way they walked along **hand in hand** and kept gazing into each other's eyes.

Underline **all** the expressions with 'in' and notice how they are used in the sentences.

Complete the column on the right to make phrases from the exercise or phrases using the following words:

error	fashion	a hurry	order	particular	practice

Space has been left for you to add your own examples.

---

1. We don't share any interests. We have nothing   in   ....

2. It was difficult but I finally did it. I did it   in   ....

3. That was a mistake. It was sent to you   in   ....

4. This is what everyone is wearing. This dress is   in   ....

5. Slow down! You're always   in   ....

6. You need a pen. Your answers must be   in   ....

7. 'Keen on' is not strong enough. She's obviously   in   ....

8. He won't be long. He'll be here   in   ....

9. Keep your papers tidy. Keep them   in   ....

10. It must hurt a lot. You can see she's   in   ....

11. I like pop music in general and rock music   in   ....

12. That's what happens nowadays. It was different   in   ....

13. The vase had been smashed. We found it   in   ....

14. She says one thing in private and another   in   ....

15. It works in theory but I'm not sure it'll work   in   ....

16. Nobody spoke. They all listened   in   ....

17. She was crying her eyes out. I found her   in   ....

18. We got there before the train left. We arrived   in   ....

....

....

Test yourself later and revise before the exam by covering the column on the right and checking how many expressions you can remember.

1.12 **Phrases** with **On** . . . .

Complete each sentence with one of the phrases below.
Use each phrase once only.

on business	**on the increase**	**on the radio**
on fire	**on his mind**	**on sale**
on foot	**on his own**	**on strike**
on guard	**on the phone**	**on time**

1. Her latest hit is .... in all good record shops.

2. He prepared the whole meal .... I offered to help, but he wanted to prove he could do it.

3. She spends hours .... talking to all her friends.

4. I've never known this bus to arrive .... **On average,** it arrives about five minutes late.

5. The staff threatened to go .... if the management did not meet their demands.

6. It looks as if the whole building is .... There are flames everywhere.

7. **On the other hand**, he could have something .... He's not really concentrating on what he's doing.

8. We had to complete the journey .... after the car ran out of petrol.

9. There was a soldier .... at the main entrance so I took a photo of him in his uniform.

10. I was listening to some music .... when there was a news flash about a plane crashing with a hundred passengers **on board**.

11. The latest figures show that crime is ...., especially in urban areas.

12. Ms Swanson is away .... at the moment, visiting one of our agents, and unfortunately her secretary is away **on holiday**.

Notice all the expressions with 'on'. Once again you see how important word partnerships are.

Complete the column on the right with phrases from the exercise and phrases with the following words:

credit   **a diet**   **loan**   **purpose**   **trial**   **his way**

Space has been left for you to add your own examples.

1.	The trip is to do with my job. I'll be away	on ....
2.	She's got two years to pay. She's buying it	on ....
3.	He has to be careful what he eats. He's	on ....
4.	I can see flames. The building must be	on ....
5.	She's going to walk. She's getting there	on ....
6.	The hall was well protected. There were soldiers	on ....
7.	More people are being attacked. Violence is	on ....
8.	Somebody's borrowed the book. It's out	on ....
9.	He's thinking about something. There's something	on ....
10.	He doesn't need any help. He can do it	on ....
11.	He's always ringing up somebody. He's always	on ....
12.	That was no accident! She did that	on ....
13.	They broadcast his speech. I heard it	on ....
14.	You can still buy it. It's still	on ....
15.	They stopped work in protest. They all went	on ....
16.	The train arrived at 7.30 as expected. It came	on ....
17.	They took her to court. They put her	on ....
18.	He's left home. He'll be here shortly. He's	on ....

....

....

Test yourself later by covering the column on the right. Can you remember all the useful expressions?

1.13 **Phrases** with **Out Of** . . . .

Complete each of the sentences with one of the phrases below.
Use each phrase once only.

out of breath	out of luck	out of reach
out of control	out of order	out of sight
out of date	out of practice	out of tune
out of doors	out of the question	out of work

1. The lift was .... so we had to use the stairs.

2. I watched them until they went .... behind a hedge.

3. It only takes one person to sing .... and the whole performance is ruined.

4. This catalogue is .... so the information about prices is no longer correct.

5. He says he's .... but I don't think he was ever any good at tennis!

6. She's been .... for over a year now and she's almost given up hope of ever finding a job.

7. I'm afraid you're .... ! I sold the last copy five minutes ago.

8. The steering wouldn't work and the tractor went .... and crashed into the wall.

9. Those children should be ...., in the fresh air, instead of in here, watching television.

10. It's .... ! I can't possibly lend you any more!

11. You get .... just climbing the stairs! You really must do some exercises to get fit!

12. It is essential to put all medicines .... on a high shelf so that small children can't get to them.

Complete the column on the right to make phrases from the exercise, or phrases using the following words:

danger   **debt**   **fashion**   **place**   **print**   **season**

Space has been left for you to add your own examples.

---

1.   I'm so unfit. After any kind of effort I get   out of   ....

2.   I couldn't steer the car properly. It was   out of   ....

3.   We were safe. We were   out of   ....

4.   That's old news. That news is   out of   ....

5.   I've repaid the money I owe so I'm finally   out of   ....

6.   Don't stay inside all day. Spend some time   out of   ....

7.   People wore that LAST year. This year it's   out of   ....

8.   There isn't any left. How unfortunate. You're   out of   ....

9.   The lift doesn't work. It's   out of   ....

10.   It's not where it should be. It's   out of   ....

11.   I haven't played tennis for ages. I'm   out of   ....

12.   The book isn't published any more. It's   out of   ....

13.   We'd never do that kind of thing. It's   out of   ....

14.   She wasn't tall enough to get it. It was   out of   ....

15.   You won't find cherries now. They're   out of   ....

16.   I can't see her. She's   out of   ....

17.   The singing was awful. I'm sure somebody was   out of   ....

18.   With all this unemployment lots of people are   out of   ....

....

....

....

....

3*

1.14 **Prepositional Phrases** . . . .

Complete each phrase below by using one of the following prepositions:

at	by	for	from	under	without

.... accident	.... first	.... now on
.... age	.... guarantee	.... present
.... air	.... the impression	.... sale
.... control	.... instance	.... times
.... far	.... least	.... warning

Now use each of the phrases above once only to complete the following sentences.

1. He was .... that we were going out together. Whatever gave him that idea?

2. Is there anything non-alcoholic - orange juice .... ?

3. I'm sure he broke the window .... He can't have done it on purpose.

4. He usually travels .... as it's much quicker.

5. .... I hated maths but later I got quite keen on it.

6. She was .... but she managed to get into the club because she looks much older than she really is.

7. The television is still .... so there was no charge.

8. We saw a new house .... at quite a reasonable price.

9. Suddenly, ..., the door burst open and she rushed in.

10. There aren't any vacancies .... but there should be some in a week or two.

11. We expect .... 200 people to turn up but there could be a lot more.

12. This is .... the cheapest holiday we've ever been on. We usually pay much more.

13. Usually the heat doesn't bother me but .... it can get pretty unbearable.

14. A new system starts today. .... all latecomers have to wait in the canteen until the next lesson starts.

15. You must keep that dog .... as we go across the fields or he'll chase after the sheep.

Put the phrases from the exercises into the appropriate list.
Add one of the prepositions to the words below to make more phrases to add to your lists.
Space has been left for your own examples.

| .... **any rate** | .... **delay** | .... **mistake** | .... **time to time** |
| .... **all means** | .... **doubt** | .... **pressure** | .... **the time being** |

AT	BY	FOR
....	....	....
....	....	....
....	....	....
....	....	....
....	....	....
....	....	....
....	....	....
....	....	....

FROM	UNDER	WITHOUT
....	....	....
....	....	....
....	....	....
....	....	....
....	....	....
....	....	....

Make sentences with any phrases you are not sure about so that you can understand and remember them.

1.15 **Word Partnerships** . . . . REVISION

Complete each of the blanks with one word only.

By (1).............................. the most terrifying day of my life was the day I met my girlfriend's family. Her father (2).............................. to her going out with somebody he had never met and insisted (3).............................. meeting me to see if he approved (4).............................. his daughter's "young man".

I spent hours getting (5).............................. for the dreaded event. I spent so long trying to choose clothes suitable (6).............................. the occasion that I (7).............................. the bus and had to (8).............................. my way to my girlfriend's house (9).............................. foot.

I had been instructed to be there for afternoon tea at three o'clock and as I did not want to be (10).............................. for this first meeting, I ran the last 500 metres. As I (11).............................. the corner of the street where her house was situated, I took a quick (12).............................. at my watch. It was five to three. I was just (13).............................. time.

My girlfriend, Sandra, opened the door, startled to see me out of (14).............................. because I had been running. The family (15).............................. barked an unfriendly welcome at me but she told me not to (16).............................. any attention as he was quite friendly, really.

I'm sure my heart was (17).............................. twice as fast as I went into the house. I was shown into a room which was so dark that (18).............................. first it was impossible to make out who was inside. Gradually, I became (19).............................. of four figures standing by a table. They stared at me (20).............................. silence. There was no escape. I was doomed.

PHRASAL VERBS 2

Phrasal verbs are very common in English, so understanding what they mean can help you in all papers in the First Certificate, for example in the Reading in Paper 1.

Phrasal verbs also appear in the blank-filling exercises in Paper 3 (Use of English) in a question such as:

> The business was so successful that they took (8)................... extra staff.

In one exercise you have to supply the missing word yourself, and in the other you are given a choice:

> 8.   **A** on   **B** off   **C** over   **D** up

where **A** is the correct answer.

A knowledge of phrasal verbs is also useful for the re-writing exercise in Paper 3, for example:

> I can't wait to see them again.
> **forward**
>
> I'm really .... them again.

where the missing words are **looking forward to seeing**.

As you do the exercises in this section, see if you can find meanings for the various particles. It will not always be possible, but it will help you to understand and remember many of the verbs that you meet.

2.1 **Phrasal Verbs** with **Up – 1** . . . .

Complete each of the groups of sentences by using the correct form of the verbs given and the particle **up**. Use each verb once only.

EXERCISE 1   **beat**   **blow**   **brush**   **call**   **clear**   **go**   **speak**   **turn**

---

1. They needed the explosives to .... a railway bridge.

2. The thieves .... him .... and stole all his money.

3. That's the third time train fares have .... this year!

4. There you are at last! I was wondering when you'd .... !

5. You'll have to .... because he's a bit deaf.

6. I went on a course to .... my German.

7. You've got my phone number, so .... me .... any time you're in the neighbourhood.

8. Don't forget to .... all this mess before you go to bed.

EXERCISE 2   **back**   **catch**   **come**   **dress**   **get**   **mix**   **stay**   **sum**

---

1. When I'm on holiday, I can lie in bed and .... when I feel like it.

2. It's a formal dinner so you'll have to .... for it.

3. I'll only complain if the others agree to .... me ....

4. Their parents said they could .... and watch the late-night film.

5. I was standing at the bus stop when a man .... and asked me the way to the station.

6. He joined the course late and had difficulty ....

7. So to .... then, we need money urgently.

8. The two boys looked so similar that I kept .... them ....

Have you checked that you used the correct form of the verb? That is very important in the exam.

Complete the first column below using the verbs from the exercises.
If you meet any other verbs that you find difficult to understand and remember, add them to the list.

1. .... **up**   **give someone support and help**

2. .... **up**   **hit or kick someone and hurt them badly**

3. .... **up**   **destroy something with an explosion**

4. .... **up**   **improve your knowledge and skill**

5. .... **up**   **phone somebody**

6. .... **up**   **get to the same standard as the others**

7. .... **up**   **tidy, to put away**

8. .... **up**   **approach someone**

9. .... **up**   **put on smart, elegant or formal clothes**

10. .... **up**   **start the day!**

11. .... **up**   **increase**

12. .... **up**   **not know the difference**

13. .... **up**   **talk in a loud, clear voice**

14. .... **up**   **not go to bed**

15. .... **up**   **list the main points**

16. .... **up**   **arrive**

.... **up**   ....

.... **up**   ....

.... **up**   ....

Test yourself by covering the verbs and looking at the definitions. Can you remember the verb? This is a good way to test yourself before the exam.

2.2 **Phrasal Verbs** with **Up – 2** . . . .

Complete each of the groups of sentences by using the correct form of the verbs given and the particle **up**. Use each verb once only.

EXERCISE 1   add   build   bundle   eat   grow   light   own   shoot

---

1. He'll only get an ice cream if he .... all his vegetables!

2. If the culprit hadn't ...., everybody would still think that it was you who set fire to the building.

3. Their eyes .... when she mentioned chocolate biscuits.

4. It's so expensive now! Prices have really .... !

5. It's taken years for her to .... the business to what it is today.

6. Not many children want to .... to be teachers.

7. After I've .... all the figures, I'll see if my total is the same as yours.

8. I've .... the magazines and tied them with string so that you can carry them more easily.

EXERCISE 2   **brighten**   **bring**   **cheer**   **draw**   **hang**   **look**   **pile**   **turn**

---

1. If there's a word that you don't understand, ... it .... in your dictionary.

2. It will be dull at first but the weather should .... in the afternoon.

3. Despite all our efforts to .... him ...., he still looks as miserable as ever.

4. Work really .... while I was away for those two days.

5. A large car .... and a tall well-dressed man stepped out.

6. Unfortunately, the caller .... before I could ask him for his number so that you could ring him back.

7. After my parents died, I was .... by my aunts.

8. Could you .... the radio .... a bit? I want to listen to the weather forecast.

Although many phrasal verbs can be used with a variety of nouns, the verbs in the exercises opposite form partnerships with a restricted number of words.
The verb **draw up**, for example, meaning *to come to a place and stop*, can only be used to talk about some kind of vehicle.

EXERCISE 1   Match each noun on the left with a phrasal verb on the right.
Use each item once only. Put your answers in the boxes provided.

1.	The caller	a.	brightened up.
2.	A car	b.	drew up.
3.	The children	c.	grew up.
4.	The culprit	d.	hung up.
5.	Her eyes	e.	lit up.
6.	Prices	f.	owned up.
7.	The weather	g.	piled up.
8.	Work	h.	shot up.

1	
2	
3	
4	
5	
6	
7	
8	

EXERCISE 2   Now do the same with the phrasal verbs on the left and the nouns on the right.

1.	add up	a.	a business
2.	bring up	b.	children
3.	build up	c.	your dinner
4.	bundle up	d.	the figures
5.	cheer up	e.	the newspapers
6.	eat up	f.	information
7.	look up	g.	who's unhappy
8.	turn up	h.	the volume

1	
2	
3	
4	
5	
6	
7	
8	

Check your memory by covering the column with the verbs. Look at the words in the other column and see if you can remember the verb that is used in each partnership.

2.3 **Phrasal Verbs** with **Up – 3** . . . .

Complete each of the groups of sentences by using the correct form of the verbs given and the particle **up**. Use each verb once only.

EXERCISE 1 **do** **give** **hold** **make** **pick** **put** **set** **take**

---

1. I'll .... you .... outside your office at six o'clock.

2. The traffic was .... because of an accident.

3. He didn't .... much of a fight, did he!

4. Is he coming or isn't he? I wish he'd .... his mind!

5. He helped his sister to .... the buttons of her cardigan.

6. You're supposed to .... your seat if an elderly or disabled person gets on the bus.

7. My dress is too long so I'll have to .... it ....

8. After he went bankrupt, he tried to .... a new business in his wife's name.

EXERCISE 2 **do** **give** **hold** **make** **pick** **put** **set** **take**

---

1. The robbers .... the bank and got away with over a quarter of a million pounds.

2. I .... golf after the doctor told me I should get more exercise.

3. I'm sure she .... that story about being in a film!

4. This house looks so much better now they've .... it ....

5. The hotels are full, so could you .... me .... for a couple of nights?

6. I .... smoking in May and haven't had a cigarette since.

7. I .... a few words of Japanese when I went there on holiday last year.

8. The police have .... road blocks throughout the area to prevent the kidnappers from escaping.

Did you notice that the phrasal verbs in the exercises on the opposite page had more than one meaning?
Complete each of the partnerships below with one of the eight phrasal verbs from the exercises. Use each verb once only.
If you are not sure of the meaning of a word partnership, check it in your dictionary.

1. .... **a business**
an inquiry
road blocks

5. .... **a hobby**
a skirt
a collection

2. .... **a passenger**
some Italian
support

6. .... **smoking**
a job
your seat

3. .... **a button**
a present
an old house

7. .... **the traffic**
a bank
someone as an example

4. .... **a story**
an excuse
your mind

8. .... **a friend for the night**
a fight
prices

STUDY TIP To revise these partnerships, first cover the left-hand column and see if you can remember the phrasal verb that goes with the group of words on the right.
Next, cover the groups of words and see how many you can remember when you look at the verbs.

2.4 **Phrasal Verbs** with **Down – 1** . . . .

Complete each sentence with the correct form of one of the verbs given and the particle **down**. Use each verb once only.

EXERCISE 1   **cut**   **die**   **jot**   **let**   **live**   **mark**   **play**   **slow**

---

1. He promised he'd come! How could he .... me .... like this?

2. After the noise had ...., he made his announcement.

3. The examiners will .... you .... if your handwriting is difficult to read.

4. .... ! There is a speed limit, you know!

5. I'll just .... my phone number on the back of the card.

6. This is so embarrassing! I'll never .... it ....

7. If you can't stop smoking entirely, please try to ....

8. They tried to .... the number of casualties to make the incident appear less serious than it really was.

EXERCISE 2   **back**   **close**   **get**   **lay**   **pour**   **run**   **settle**   **shout**

---

1. The battery has .... so the car won't start.

2. They had .... some very strict rules about who was eligible to join their society.

3. I tried to speak but I was .... by some of the audience.

4. They finally .... and agreed to make the changes that we had suggested.

5. Having so much work to do is really .... me ....

6. When are you going to .... and find a job?

7. The rain .... all morning so we stayed indoors.

8. Last month another shop .... because business was so bad.

Complete each blank in the column on the left with a suitable verb from the exercises.
Space has been left for you to add your own examples.

1.	**down**	withdraw your objections
2.	**down**	stop all work, cease trading
3.	**down**	do something less often
4.	**down**	become quieter
5.	**down**	annoy, make unhappy
6.	**down**	make a note of
7.	**down**	establish rules
8.	**down**	disappoint, not keep a promise
9.	**down**	make people forget a mistake
10.	**down**	give a lower grade
11.	**down**	make something appear less important
12.	**down**	come down heavily (of rain)
13.	**down**	lose power
14.	**down**	live a quiet, routine life
15.	**down**	not allow to be heard
16.	**down**	go less fast
....	**down**	....
....	**down**	....
....	**down**	....
....	**down**	....

Test yourself by covering the column on the left and trying to remember the phrasal verbs.

2.5 **Phrasal Verbs** with **Down – 2** . . . .

Complete each sentence with the correct form of one of the verbs given and the particle **down**. Use each verb once only.

EXERCISE 1   **break**   **bring**   **come**   **go**   **knock**   **put**   **take**   **turn**

---

1. The car went out of control and .... a pedestrian.

2. I've .... a deposit of £2,000 on a new car.

3. The competition has forced them to .... their prices.

4. The engine was on fire and the plane had to .... in that field over there.

5. We didn't expect him to .... such a good offer.

6. Unfortunately, the car .... at the crossroads.

7. The news of job losses hasn't .... very well.

8. He listened carefully and .... all the particulars in his note book.

EXERCISE 2   **break**   **bring**   **come**   **go**   **knock**   **put**   **take**   **turn**

---

1. .... the radio .... ! We can hear it all over the house!

2. The President used tanks to .... the rebellion.

3. After you've .... the tent you have to fold it up.

4. The opposition parties hoped to .... the government.

5. She .... in tears when she heard the news.

6. They're going to .... the old cinema .... and build an office block in its place.

7. When I woke up next morning, the swelling had ....

8. The rain .... so heavily that we were forced to shelter for a while.

Complete each of the groups of partnerships below with one of the phrasal verbs from the exercise. Use each verb once only.

1. ....
    a building
    a pedestrian

2. ....
    the volume
    an invitation
    most of the candidates

3. ....
    their prices
    enemy missiles
    the government

4. ....
    a deposit
    a rebellion
    (an animal)

5. ....
    a tent
    information
    the decorations

6. **We didn't expect the rain to** .... **so heavily.**
    The price of eggs has
    Where did the plane

7.   **How did the news** ....
    When will this swelling
    Let's watch the sun

8.   **Where did your car** ....
    The bad news made him
    Why did the marriage

2.6 **Phrasal Verbs** with **Out – 1** . . . .

Complete each of the groups of sentences by using the correct form of the verbs given and the particle **out**.
Use each verb once only.

EXERCISE 1   **back**   **break**   **burn**   **eat**   **leave**   **point**   **sort**   **stand**

---

1. He had agreed to open the show and then he .... at the last moment saying he wanted more money.

2. She .... that he was the only person who hadn't come.

3. The prisoners .... while the guards were asleep.

4. We rarely .... as the restaurants are so expensive.

5. We had to .... everything .... into different sizes.

6. They waited until the fire had .... before examining what was left of the house.

7. With those clothes she'll certainly .... in a crowd!

8. I'll check through the list in case I've .... anything ....

EXERCISE 2   **find**   **hand**   **get**   **look**   **pass**   **run**   **shoot**   **wear**

---

1. He should .... more and not sit at home feeling miserable.

2. When our supply of coal .... we had to burn wood instead.

3. She .... because the room was so stuffy.

4. They followed him from work to .... where he lived.

5. You'll .... yourself .... doing all this extra work!

6. Suddenly the front door opened, and a small boy .... and ran down the street.

7. The examiner will now .... the question papers.

8. .... ! There's a car coming!

Complete the first column below using the verbs from the exercise.
If you find any other verbs that you find difficult to understand and remember, add them to your list.

1.	out	not do as promised
2.	out	stop burning
3.	out	escape from prison
4.	out	go for a meal in a restaurant
5.	out	discover information
6.	out	go to places and meet people
7.	out	distribute
8.	out	not include
9.	out	be careful
10.	out	lose consciousness
11.	out	draw attention to something
12.	out	be all used up
13.	out	appear suddenly
14.	out	separate into categories
15.	out	be very noticeable
16.	out	make very tired
....	out	....
....	out	....
....	out	....
....	out	....

Test yourself by covering the verb column and reading the definitions.

4*

2.7 **Phrasal Verbs** with **Out – 2** . . . .

Complete each of the groups of sentences by using the correct forms of the verbs given and the particle **out.**
Use each verb once only.

EXERCISE 1   **break**   **bring**   **die**   **fall**   **pull**   **rule**   **run**   **walk**

---

1. I was driving down the road when a car suddenly .... in front of me.

2. The acting was so terrible that half the audience ....

3. The tradition had .... but it was revived to attract tourists to the town.

4. In this hot weather a fire could .... almost anywhere.

5. They've .... a new range of cosmetics for teenagers.

6. It must be serious to make such close friends ....

7. We had to hurry because time was ....

8. We can't .... the possibility of more rain, I'm afraid.

EXERCISE 2   **burst**   **carry**   **check**   **cross**   **drop**   **sit**   **wash**   **work**

---

1. It's difficult to .... exactly how much money to take.

2. You must .... the instructions exactly as printed.

3. Remember to use your ruler to .... any mistakes.

4. This new miracle powder will .... even the most stubborn stains, leaving your clothes fresh and clean.

5. We .... laughing when we saw how ridiculous he looked.

6. I think I'll .... this dance .... and rest my feet.

7. Hotel guests have to .... by 11 o'clock in the morning.

8. Some competitors were forced to .... because conditions were so bad.

The verbs in the exercises opposite form partnerships with a restricted number of words. The verb **work out,** for example, is usually followed only by words like **answer, solution** etc.

EXERCISE 1   Match each noun on the left with a phrasal verb on the right. Use each item once only. Put your answers in the boxes provided.

---

1. Some of the audience	a. broke out.	**1**
2. A car	b. checked out.	**2**
3. One contestant	c. died out.	**3**
4. A fire	d. dropped out.	**4**
5. The friends	e. fell out.	**5**
6. The hotel guests	f. pulled out.	**6**
7. Time	g. ran out.	**7**
8. The tradition	h. walked out.	**8**

EXERCISE 2   Now do the same with the phrasal verb on the left and the noun on the right.

---

1. bring out	a. the right answer	**1**
2. burst out	b. crying	**2**
3. carry out	c. this dance	**3**
4. cross out	d. dirt/a stain	**4**
5. rule out	e. instructions	**5**
6. sit out	f. any mistakes	**6**
7. wash out	g. a possibility	**7**
8. work out	h. a new product	**8**

Check your memory by covering the column with the verbs.
Look at the words in the other column and see if you can remember the verb that is used in each partnership.

2.8 **Phrasal Verbs** with **Out – 3** . . . .

Complete each of the groups of sentences by using the correct forms of the verbs given and the particle **out**. Use each verb once only.

EXERCISE 1 **come** **go** **let** **make** **put** **set** **take** **turn**

---

1. My boyfriend is .... me .... to the cinema this evening.

2. Her latest film is due to .... next month.

3. It was so dark that they could hardly .... where the exit was.

4. As the water hit him, he .... a startled cry.

5. The fire was so fierce that it took ages to .... it ....

6. There was a power cut and all the lights ....

7. The talk .... to be more interesting than I'd expected.

8. It wasn't until 2.30 that we finally .... on our trip.

EXERCISE 2 **break** **bring** **come** **go** **knock** **put** **take** **turn**

---

1. The only library books he ever .... are detective novels.

2. He .... he was deaf so that people wouldn't keep asking him for money.

3. The stain still hasn't .... even though I followed the instructions very carefully.

4. She .... a statement to the press saying that she and her husband had agreed to separate.

5. I had to .... the dress a bit, especially round the waist.

6. We were surprised that so many spectators .... for the game after last week's terrible performance.

7. In this document, we have .... our proposals in a clear and concise way so that everyone can understand them.

8. At low tide, the sea .... a long way.

Complete each of the groups of partnerships below with one of the phrasal verbs from the exercises. Use each verb once only.

1. ....
the light
the cat for the night
a press statement

2. ....
the prisoners for some exercise
a scream
my trousers as I've put on weight

3. ....
my ideas in this book
on our walk
to teach some useful vocabulary

4. ....
a book from the library
my new girlfriend
any words that might offend people

5. ....
the light
over six thousand cakes a week
to be better than expected

6. ....
you're ill to avoid going to school
what he's saying
the cheque to my wife

7. How can I make this stain .... ?
When does your new book
How did the photos

8. What made the lights .... ?
Has he really asked you to
When does the programme

To test yourself, cover one half of the partnership and see if you can remember the other half.

2.9 **Phrasal Verbs** with **Off – 1** . . . .

Complete each sentence with one of the verbs given and the particle **off.** Use each verb once only.
Make sure you use the correct form of the verb.
Notice some of the verbs need (someone) between the verb and the particle. Underline all of these verbs like <u>to tell someone off</u>, after you have done the exercise.

EXERCISE 1   **let**   **put**   **pull**   **see**   **show**   **slip**   **stop**   **write**

---

1. I'll .... the road just by that tree so that we can get out of this traffic for a while.

2. We managed to .... while they were all watching television so nobody realised we had gone.

3. Don't .... seeing your dentist until you're in agony.

4. Why don't you .... in Cambridge on your way home?

5. I wish he wouldn't .... like that! I'm not impressed!

6. I'll .... you .... with just a warning this time.

7. The whole family were at the airport to .... her ....

8. I've decided to .... and ask them for more information. You haven't got a stamp I could use, have you?

EXERCISE 2   **cut**   **drop**   **get**   **go**   **kick**   **put**   **set**   **tell**

---

1. I was trying to work but the noise kept .... me ....

2. Ask the driver to .... you .... in front of the Town Hall.

3. The teacher keeps .... her .... for talking in the lesson.

4. An operator pressed the wrong button and .... us .... so we never did finish our conversation.

5. That's him .... that bus over there!

6. The lights .... and plunged the house into darkness.

7. The noise .... the dog .... barking again.

8. The centre forward .... and within seconds most of the team were in the other half.

Complete the first column below using the verbs from the exercise.
Space has been left for you to add your own examples to the list.

1. .... off   disconnect a phone call accidentally

2. .... off   leave a passenger somewhere

3. .... off   leave a bus, train etc.

4. .... off   stop operating (electricity, a computer, TV)

5. .... off   start a game of football

6. .... off   not punish

7. .... off   drive to the side of a road

8. .... off   Two meanings: a) postpone b) distract

9. .... off   say goodbye to someone going on a journey

10. .... off   cause an activity to start

11. .... off   do things to try and impress people

12. .... off   leave quietly

13. .... off   break your journey somewhere for a time

14. .... off   reprimand

15. .... off   send a letter to an organisation

.... off   ....

.... off   ....

.... off   ....

.... off   ....

.... off   ....

Test yourself by covering the first column and trying to remember the phrasal verb.

PAPER 3

2.10 **Phrasal Verbs** with **Off – 2** . . . .

Complete each sentence with one of the verbs given and the particle **off**. Use each verb once only.
Make sure you use the correct form of the verb.

EXERCISE 1   call   drop   go   keep   shake   take   turn   wear

1. I .... in the middle of the film and woke up at the end.

2. The meeting was .... due to lack of support.

3. The bomb .... just as we were passing the Town Hall.

4. It's best to .... the subject to avoid embarrassing him.

5. Why don't you .... your jacket if you're too hot?

6. The effects of the anaesthetic should .... in a couple of hours.

7. If you smell gas, ... the supply immediately.

8. I've had this cold for weeks and I just can't .... it .... !

EXERCISE 2   fall   give   hold   lay   pay   ring   set   take

1. A plane .... or lands every two minutes at this airport.

2. He had to .... in case his boss saw him using the phone.

3. I've finally managed to .... that loan.

4. Sales of umbrellas usually .... in the summer and then pick up again in the autumn.

5. If the rain .... we'll be able to have our picnic.

6. As it got hotter, the machine .... a horrible smell.

7. If the recession continues, I'll have to .... more staff.

8. We .... down the track that led to the village.

58

The verbs in the exercises opposite form partnerships with a restricted number of nouns. Learning the complete partnership will help you to understand and remember each verb.

EXERCISE 1   Match each noun on the left with a phrasal verb on the right. Use each item once only. Put your answers in the boxes provided.

1.	The bomb	a.	dropped off.	1	
2.	The caller	b.	fell off.	2	
3.	My headache	c.	held off.	3	
4.	The plane	d.	rang off.	4	
5.	The rain	e.	set off.	5	
6.	Sales	f.	took off.	6	
7.	The sleepy man	g.	went off.	7	
8.	The travellers	h.	wore off.	8	

EXERCISE 2   Now do the same with the phrasal verb on the left and the noun on the right.

1.	call off	a.	your coat	1	
2.	give off	b.	a cold	2	
3.	keep off	c.	a loan	3	
4.	lay off	d.	a meeting	4	
5.	pay off	e.	a terrible smell	5	
6.	shake off	f.	staff	6	
7.	take off	g.	a delicate subject	7	
8.	turn off	h.	the television	8	

Test yourself by covering over one of the columns and trying to remember the other half of the partnership.

2.11 **Phrasal Verbs** with **On – 1** . . . .

Complete each sentence with the correct form of one of the verbs given and the particle **on**. Use each verb once only.

EXERCISE 1 **carry** **catch** **cheer** **hold** **pick** **send** **set** **stay**

---

1. She paused to have a drink and then .... speaking.

2. He shouldn't .... her just because she's a bit slow.

3. We don't know her new address, but her parents will .... any letters they receive for her.

4. I've decided to .... at school and take some more exams.

5. The crowd .... her .... as she overtook the race leader.

6. Leave immediately or I'll .... the dogs .... you!

7. Could you .... a minute while I get my coat?

8. I don't think this new fashion will really ....

EXERCISE 2 **count** **drag** **live** **look** **move** **switch** **touch** **try**

---

1. No wonder the video doesn't work! You haven't .... it .... !

2. I'd better .... this hat .... to see if it's the right size.

3. I'm sure I can .... you all to do your best.

4. Times were hard with only a small income to ....

5. He only .... the subject. He didn't go into it in detail.

6. Now, could we .... and discuss something which I hope will be slightly less controversial?

7. The shoppers .... in amazement as the cars sped by.

8. The meeting seemed to .... for hours and we just weren't getting anywhere.

STUDY TIP   In sentence 6 in exercise 1, **set on** has the construction **VERB + OBJECT + PARTICLE.** There are other phrasal verbs which can **only** take this construction, as well as others which use it very often. Whenever you study a phrasal verb it is important to check **exactly** how it is used.

Complete each blank in the column on the left with a suitable verb from the exercises.
Space has been left for you to add your own examples.

1.	on	continue
2.	on	become popular
3.	on	shout encouragement
4.	on	rely on
5.	on	continue unnecessarily for a long time
6.	on	wait
7.	on	have (money or food) for survival
8.	on	watch an activity
9.	on	start talking about a new subject
10.	on	repeatedly criticise
11.	on	forward (a letter etc)
12.	on	order to attack
13.	on	not leave at the expected time
14.	on	start electrical equipment
15.	on	mention briefly
16.	on	put on something to see if it fits
....	on	....
....	on	....
....	on	....
....	on	....

Test yourself by covering the column on the left and trying to remember the phrasal verbs.

2.12 **Phrasal Verbs** with **On – 2** . . . .

Complete each sentence with the correct form of one of the verbs given and the particle **on**. Use each verb once only.

EXERCISE 1 **call**   **come**   **get**   **go**   **keep**   **put**   **take**   **turn**

---

1. The noise of that cassette player is .... my nerves!

2. We'll .... some of the temporary staff .... for an extra two or three weeks.

3. There's so much to organise when you .... a play.

4. .... ! Don't worry! Everything will be all right!

5. The tap was so rusty that he couldn't .... it ....

6. I'm sorry. I interrupted you. Please ....

7. I'm .... every one of you to do your bit! We need all the help we can get!

8. We stopped at an airport in the middle of nowhere to .... some more passengers.

EXERCISE 2 **call**   **come**   **get**   **go**   **keep**   **put**   **take**   **turn**

---

1. The police haven't got much of a description to ....

2. I wish he wouldn't .... staring at me all the time.

3. I'm afraid I .... a lot of weight during my holiday.

4. Business was so good that we had to .... extra staff.

5. He's got a headache and he thinks he's got a cold ....

6. I haven't seen her for ages so I'll .... her on my way home.

7. It's a great relationship. We .... really well.

8. Suddenly the dog .... her and tried to bite her arm.

STUDY TIP   As you do the exercises in this book, make a note of any common expressions that you find. Did you notice **getting on my nerves** and **for ages**? Look through the sentences for more expressions like these.

Complete each of the groups of partnerships below with one of the phrasal verbs from the exercises. Use each verb once only.

___

1. .... the bus
   my nerves
   well with somebody

2. .... your coat
   another record
   weight

3. .... the tap
   the charm
   the radio

4. .... more staff
   a different appearance
   more responsibility

5. .... most of the staff after the Sales
   singing until he tells you to stop
   (about her new car) all the time

6. .... him on the way home
   them for support
   you all to congratulate Mike on . . . .

7.   **When will the lights** ....
   We haven't got much information to
   How long will the meeting
   Don't stop! Please

8.   **When did this headache** ....
   I'm waiting for the news to
          Oh   **You can do it!**

___

PAPER 3

2.13 **Phrasal Verbs** with **In** and **Into** . . . .

Complete each sentence with the correct form of one of the verbs given and the particle **in**.
Use each verb once only.

EXERCISE 1 **check** **flood** **hand** **join** **show** **sink** **step** **stop**

---

1. Please .... the homework that you did last night.

2. Donations have .... since she made the appeal and we've got
over a million pounds already.

3. Could you .... the next patient, Miss Frobisher?

4. What time do I have to .... for my flight?

5. It took some time for the news to .... I just couldn't believe it!

6. He'll have to .... and try to settle the dispute.

7. One guest refused to .... the game with all the others.

8. I'm .... tonight to finish writing that letter.

Complete these sentences in the same way as the exercise above but this time use the
particle **into**.

EXERCISE 2 **bump** **burst** **go** **look** **pull** **rush** **talk** **turn**

---

1. She .... tears when her father said she couldn't go.

2. The coach .... a restaurant at the side of the road and all the
passengers got out.

3. Guess who I .... on the train this morning.

4. The police are .... a series of robberies in this area.

5. They've .... the grocer's .... a small supermarket.

6. She managed to .... me .... helping her organise the party.

7. I've decided to .... the army when I leave school.

8. Marriage is a big step so you shouldn't .... it. Are you sure
you're doing the right thing?

64

Complete the first column below using the verbs from the exercises.
Space has been left for you to add your own examples to the list.

1.	....	in	register at an airport or hotel
2.	....	in	come in large numbers
3.	....	in	give somebody some work you've done
4.	....	in	take part in an activity
5.	....	in	bring somebody into a room
6.	....	in	be slowly understood
7.	....	in	get involved, intervene
8.	....	in	not go out
9.	....	into	meet by chance
10.	....	into	begin laughing or crying suddenly
11.	....	into	join an organisation
12.	....	into	investigate
13.	....	into	go off the road to break a car journey
14.	....	into	do something without thinking
15.	....	into	persuade
16.	....	into	change

....

....

....

....

....

Test yourself by covering the column on the left.

2.14 **Phrasal Verbs** with **In – 2** . . . .

Complete each of the groups of sentences by using the correct form of the verbs given and the particle **in**. Use each verb once only.

EXERCISE 1 **break** **bring** **call** **come** **fill** **get** **put** **take**

1. Could you .... on the way to work and see how she is?

2. Now he's had central heating ...., the whole house is much warmer.

3. She seemed genuine and so we were .... by her story.

4. My new job should .... an extra forty pounds a week.

5. Unfortunately the tide .... faster than they had expected and they found they were trapped.

6. I'll tell her as soon as she .... from work.

7. The thieves .... through a bedroom window and stole all her jewels.

8. The work's got to be done so we need another typist to .... while Laura's away.

EXERCISE 2 **break** **bring** **call** **come** **fill** **get** **put** **take**

1. I seem to spend all my time .... forms!

2. They were deep in conversation so I didn't like to ....

3. The government managed to .... again, but with a substantially reduced majority.

4. I've had to .... most of my clothes since I lost weight.

5. They've .... a new law making it illegal to shoot certain rare species of birds.

6. If he can't fix it, I'll .... the engineer.

7. We had to .... a lot of overtime to get the job done.

8. I'm repairing the roof to stop the rain ....

Complete each of the groups of partnerships below with one of the phrasal verbs from the exercises. Use each verb once only.

1. .... as the conversation is getting boring
   and steal her jewels
   a new pair of shoes

2. .... a form
   while the boss is away
   all the cracks

3. .... central heating
   a request for more paper
   at least forty hours a week

4. .... from work
   and drive off
   with a reduced majority

5. .... this jacket as I've lost weight
   what he is saying
   many people because he's so plausible

6. .... on the way home
   the engineer to look at it
   those machines to check for a fault

7. .... a colleague from another department
   a new law
   a considerable amount of money each year

8. This hammer should   .... useful.
   We expected him to   first or second
   When does the tide
   Don't let the rain
   This report has just

Test yourself by covering one half of the partnerships.

2.15 **Verbs** with **Other Particles – 1** . . . .

Complete each sentence with the correct form of one of the phrasal verbs given. Use each verb once only.

EXERCISE 1	come to	go with	put through	take over
	get round	press for	see through	turn away

1. That colour doesn't really .... your new dress.

2. Our firm was .... by a large multi-national company.

3. When it .... computers, she knows everything.

4. She's so good at flattery that she can .... anybody.

5. I .... him immediately. He didn't fool me for a second!

6. Applicants are .... some tests to check their fitness.

7. The employees are .... a much bigger pay increase.

8. The stadium was full so some of the fans were ....

EXERCISE 2	bring round	get away	hear from	see to
	come across	get by	pull through	take after

1. My salary isn't very high but we manage to ....

2. I've finally .... Mary. The letter arrived yesterday.

3. With that bad temper she certainly .... her father. He's exactly the same!

4. Could you .... the vegetables while I prepare the meat?

5. I poured water over him to .... him .... after he'd fainted.

6. He was seriously ill but he managed to ....

7. She .... her old pullover while tidying up the cupboard.

8. The thief managed to .... by running through a crowd.

Complete the column on the left with the verbs from the exercises opposite. Use each verb once only.
Space has been left for you to add your own examples.

___

1. .... revive

2. .... find by chance

3. .... be a question of, concern

4. .... escape

5. .... just manage to continue your life

6. .... persuade 🯅 to do something

7. .... match, suit

8. .... receive a letter or phone call

9. .... try hard to get

10. .... recover

11. .... make 🯅 do a test

12. .... realise what 🯅 is really like

13. .... deal with, do something about

14. .... resemble

15. .... get control of

16. .... refuse entry

....

....

....

....

___

Test yourself by covering the column on the left.

___

2.16 **Verbs** with **Other Particles – 2** . . . .

Complete each sentence with the correct form of one of the phrasal verbs given. Use each verb once only.

EXERCISE 1	**brush aside**	**leap at**	**put by**	**stick to**
	fish for	**pay back**	**run over**	**toy with**

---

1. You could see she was .... compliments about her new hat but I think it looked terrible.

2. I've got a little money .... in case of emergencies.

3. The car went up on the pavement and .... a pedestrian.

4. I'll .... my promise and take her to the cinema even though I hate horror films.

5. He's .... the idea of organising a sports day but it's not definite yet.

6. How can I possibly .... all the money I owe?

7. We expected him to .... the chance to have a few days off but he didn't seem at all enthusiastic.

8. She .... all our objections and bought a video camera.

EXERCISE 2	**attend to**	**cut back**	**get at**	**stand for**
	bring back	**fall for**	**run through**	**take back**

---

1. Maybe I'd better .... the plan again to make sure we all know what we're supposed to be doing.

2. He's going to .... election as an independent candidate.

3. It was very difficult to .... the truth because nobody wanted to tell us anything about what happened that day.

4. I .... what I said. This show isn't as bad as I expected.

5. Fancy him .... such an old trick! I bet he feels stupid!

6. Could you .... this customer? I'm rather busy at the moment.

7. If we don't sell more, we'll have to .... production.

8. That song always .... memories of the time we went on a package holiday to Spain.

Many of these sentences contain three-word partnerships. Can you find and underline them all?

The verbs on the left are followed by a restricted number of nouns. The expression **fish for compliments** is a good example of this. Remember to look out for partnerships like this.

EXERCISE 1   Match the verb on the left with a suitable item on the right.
Use each item once only. Write your answers in the boxes provided.

1.	attend to	a.	a customer	1	
2.	fall for	b.	election	2	
3.	pay back	c.	an idea	3	
4.	run over	d.	the money I owe	4	
5.	stand for	e.	a pedestrian	5	
6.	stick to	f.	my promise	6	
7.	take back	g.	a trick	7	
8.	toy with	h.	what I said	8	

EXERCISE 2   Now do the same with these partnerships.

1.	bring back	a.	compliments	1	
2.	brush aside	b.	memories	2	
3.	cut back	c.	some money	3	
4.	fish for	d.	any objections	4	
5.	get at	e.	an opportunity/chance	5	
6.	leap at	f.	a plan/scheme/proposal	6	
7.	put by	g.	production	7	
8.	run through	h.	the truth	8	

Test yourself by covering one of the columns.

2.17 **Verbs** with **Other Particles – 3**. . . . .

Each of the phrasal verbs below has more than one meaning. Use them in the correct form to complete the sentences. Use each verb once only in each exercise.

EXERCISE 1

| call for | come over | give away | put forward |
| come round | get over | go through | stand by |

---

1. It took me a long time to .... my uncle's death.

2. The film starts at seven so I'll .... you at six thirty.

3. I've got a proposal to .... at tomorrow's meeting.

4. It took him quite some time to .... after he'd fainted.

5. A real friend will always .... you if you're in trouble.

6. We have to .... a series of warm-up exercises first.

7. You must .... for a meal some time.

8. At the age of sixty-three he suddenly .... most of his money and went to live on a remote island.

EXERCISE 2 Use the same verbs with these sentences.

---

1. The clocks have to be .... by one hour tonight so we won't get so much sleep.

2. Extra police are .... in case there's any trouble.

3. He managed to .... his ideas .... in a clear and concise way.

4. She has always .... as somebody who knows what she's doing.

5. He has never .... the secret of his marvellous pastry.

6. Apparently, all children .... a stage of taking no notice of what their parents say.

7. The protesters are .... immediate action to deal with the increase in crimes of violence.

8. He's a stubborn man but I'm sure she'll make him ...., especially when he realises there's money to be made.

Complete each of the word partnerships with one of the phrasal verbs from the exercises opposite. Use each verb once only.

---

1. .... free samples
   our secret
   all his money

2. .... her when she's in trouble
   my original decision
   in case we need you

3. .... on the way
   immediate action
   a change of plan

4. .... for a meal some time next week
   from a rival organisation
   as a very pleasant person

5. .... his illnesses
   the shock of her leaving him
   the idea that we'll all benefit

6. .... a surprise candidate
   the meeting to earlier in the week
   an alternative proposal

7. .... with some more coffee
   after a lot of persuasion
   after being knocked out

8. .... all your notes before the exam
   the official channels
   a stage of not caring what they wear

Test youself from time to time by covering over either part of each partnership and checking what you can remember. This is useful revision just before your exam.

2.18 **Three-Word Verbs – 1** . . . .

Each of the two-word verbs below exist on their own as phrasal verbs. Turn them into three-word verbs by adding **for, of, on** or **with**.

---

back out ....   **cut down** ....   **run out** ....

carry on ....   **drop out** ....   **stand in** ....

catch up ....   **fit in** ....

catch up ....   **look back** ....

Now use each of the three-word verbs you have formed to complete the sentences. Use each verb once only. Make sure you use the correct form of the verb.

---

1. Unfortunately, the team had to .... the competition because of injuries.

2. He's signed a contract so if he tries to .... the agreement he made, we'll take him to court.

3. He was travelling so slowly that we soon .... him.

4. If you really want to slim, you can start by .... the amount of cakes and chocolate you eat!

5. I felt that I didn't really .... the rest of the team so I decided that I'd better move.

6. I've got some reading to .... so I'm afraid I can't come out tonight.

7. When I .... the incident now, I can't understand what all the fuss was about.

8. The boss was ill so his assistant had to .... him.

9. It started raining so heavily that we couldn't .... the match.

10. We've .... beans so would you like peas instead?

Did you notice what kinds of words go with the three-word verbs you have studied in the exercise? Look back at the exercise and underline all the useful word partnerships.

Complete the verb in each of the partnerships.

1. back   ....   an agreement
                                           an arrangement

2. carry   ....   what you're doing
                                           our conversation

3. catch   ....   her at the end of the road
                                           the rest of the class

4. catch   ....   all that work I should have done
                                           some sleep

5. cut   ....   smoking
                                           the number of sweets you eat

6. drop   ....   the competition
                                           college

7. fit   ....   his plans
                                           the rest of the team
                                           whatever suits you best

8. look   ....   all those good times we had together
                                           the time when I ...

9. run   ....   time
                                           excuses
                                           sugar

10. stand ....   the star and do this stunt
                                           a colleague who is ill

Test yourself by covering either the phrasal verbs or what follows them.

2.19 **Three-Word Verbs – 2** . . . .

Complete each sentence by using a particle from the list on the left and one from the list on the right to make a three-word verb.

You can use the particles more than once but you have to make a different three-word verb each time.

| away back down | | for on |
| in round through up | | to with |

1. They came .... a lot of criticism for the way they ran the company.

2. She's come .... a wonderful idea for getting publicity.

3. We've done .... the old system of issuing tickets. It's all done by computers nowadays.

4. He refuses to face .... the fact that he's no longer as young and fit as he used to be.

5. I really don't feel .... going out this evening. I've got a splitting headache.

6. We have our old machine to fall .... if ever the new one breaks down.

7. Why are the children so quiet? They must be getting .... something!

8. She's finally got .... answering my letter after all this time!

9. He's gone .... some kind of virus, so he won't be coming.

10. She went .... her promise even though she knew we were all relying on her.

11. I don't go .... sport very much apart from the occasional game of tennis.

12. Surely he won't go .... the plan. It's much too risky.

Now underline all the three-word verbs you have made. Look carefully at the words which follow them.

Complete the column on the left with the verbs from the exercise opposite. Space has been left for you to add your own verbs.

1. .... receive (criticism)

2. .... think of an idea

3. .... abolish

4. .... accept and deal with (a difficulty)

5. .... feel able to do something

6. .... use instead

7. .... do something you aren't happy about

8. .... finally do something after a long delay

9. .... catch some kind of illness

10. .... not keep (a promise)

11. .... do regularly (eg a sport)

12. .... complete something you've agreed to do

....

....

....

....

....

....

....

....

Test yourself by covering the column on the left.

2.20 Three-Word Verbs – 3 . . . .

Use one particle from the list on the left and one from the list on the right to complete each sentence.

down forward	for of
in out up	on to with

1. Thumb-sucking is a habit most children grow .... fairly soon.

2. She always listens to the news in order to keep .... what's happening.

3. You would have thought she would let me .... the secret! I am supposed to be her best friend!

4. The show will have to be really good to live .... all the advance publicity.

5. I want people to look .... me, not treat me as if I was some kind of fool.

6. They were very snobbish. They looked .... anyone they thought came from the wrong part of town.

7. I'm looking .... going to the concert next Friday. It should be really good.

8. He took her to the best restaurant in town to make .... keeping her waiting for so long.

9. I just couldn't put .... the noise any more so I banged on the wall.

10. He's old enough to stand .... himself now! I can't always be there to hold his hand!

11. It takes courage to stand .... somebody who's bigger and stronger than you are.

12. He doesn't have to take it .... us just because his wonderful plan didn't work!

Now underline the three-word verbs and look carefully at the words which follow them. Notice the special expression in number 3.

Complete the verbs in each of the partnerships.

---

1. grow   ....   such childish behaviour
                                                   that habit

2. keep   ....   the rest of the class
                                                   all the latest gossip
                                                   the race leaders

3. let 👤   ....   what's going on
                                                   the secret

4. live   ....   my expectations
                                                   its reputation for excellence

5. look   ....   'ordinary' workers
                                                   anybody from the poor part of town
                                                   people without qualifications

6. look   ....   hearing from you
                                                   seeing you all again soon
                                                   tomorrow night's concert

7. look   ....   people who had an expensive car
                                                   her as a role model

8. make   ....   forgetting about your birthday
                                                   all the times I've let you down
                                                   the trouble he's caused

9. put   ....   such a boring speech
                                                   all that noise
                                                   looking at her holiday photos

10. stand ....   yourself
                                                   your rights
                                                   what you believe in

11. stand ....   the stresses of everyday life
                                                   that bully
                                                   almost constant use

12. take it ....   the dog although it's not his fault
                                                   other people when I get upset

---

Test yourself by either covering the verbs or what follows them.
Remember to revise like this before the exam.

2.21 **Phrasal Verbs** . . . . REVISION

Use the word given and other words to complete the second sentence so that it means the same as the first one. You must use between two and five words, including the word given.

---

1. I haven't smoked for over three years now.
   gave
   I .... over three years ago.

2. The meeting has been postponed until next Friday.
   put
   They .... until next Friday.

3. There isn't any sugar left.
   run
   We've .... sugar.

4. His recovery was slow.
   get
   It took him a long .... his illness.

5. What was the reason for their late arrival?
   turn
   Why did .... so late?

6. You can stay here for the night.
   put
   I can .... here for the night.

7. You'll have to make the speech instead of Brian.
   stand
   You'll have to .... and make the speech.

8. It took them ages to answer my letter.
   round
   They didn't .... my letter for ages.

9. That noise is driving me crazy!
   put
   I can't .... that noise any longer!

10. He feels superior because he's so rich.
    looks
    He .... other people because he's so rich.

11. We've got a spare generator in case of emergency.
    fall
    We've got another generator to .... in case of emergency.

12. I didn't want to be the only one to complain.
    backed
    If someone .... I would have complained.

WORD FORMATION 3

A good way to increase your vocabulary is to see if you can find other forms of a word you already know. You need to think of grammatically different words and both positive and negative words. If you look in a dictionary, you can often find these other forms in or near the original word.

If you consider the word **imagine**, for example, you should also learn:

imaginable   imaginary   imaginative(ly)   imagination

Do any of these words have a negative form? You can check this by looking up the prefixes **dis-, il-, im-, in-, non-** and **un-**. By doing this, you should find the words **unimaginable** and **unimaginative.**

In Paper 3 you have to do an exercise in which you complete a passage with the correct forms of the words given, for example:

It was raining (60)...................... as the helicopter continued   HEAVY

to bring all the (61)...................... to the shore. The pilot's task   SURVIVE

was made worse by the (62)...................... weather conditions.   PREDICT

The first word describes how it rained, so you need the adverb **heavily.**

In the second blank you need the **plural** noun **survivors.**

The third missing word describes the weather conditions, so you need an adjective. However, from the sentence it is clear that you need the **negative** adjective **unpredictable.**

It is therefore very important to think very carefully about what kind of word you have to put in the sentence and to try and learn **all** the forms of a word.

If you make sentences using the different forms of a word, this will help you to understand and remember them more easily.

3.1 **Word Formation: Adjectives – 1** . . . .

Form the adjective and its antonym (opposite) with **in-** or **un-**.

	ADJECTIVE	OPPOSITE		ADJECTIVE	OPPOSITE
attention	....	....	**health**	....	....
attract	....	....	**offend**	....	....
comfort	....	....	**predict**	....	....
competence	....	....	**reason**	....	....
formality	....	....	**rely**	....	....

Now use each negative adjective to fill a suitable blank.

1. My watch is very .... so I'm not sure of the correct time.

2. If that chair is ...., try this one over here.

3. The atmosphere was very .... and everyone was on first-name terms.

4. He was so .... that he sent everybody the wrong information.

5. Was it .... of me to expect them to do so much homework?

6. That terrible make-up makes her look most ....

7. He was a very .... pupil and seemed to spend most of the time looking out of the window.

8. He keeps saying that eating all this fast food is ...., especially if you don't get much exercise.

9. He's very .... You never know what he's going to do next.

10. I thought it was an .... remark but apparently she was deeply insulted.

> **STUDY TIP** When you do a word transformation exercise, you will nearly always find some sentences where you need a negative form of the word.
> When you make lists of adjectives, always put the negative form, if there is one.

IN- OR **UN-** ?

Form the antonym of each of the adjectives in the list below and put them into the appropriate column. Put the 'root word' in front of each adjective.

.....believable   .....decisive   .....excusable   .....expensive   .....fortunate
.....helpful   .....profitable   .....sensitive   .....considerate   .....successful

Think about the 'root word' from which the adjective can be formed. Sometimes this will be a noun, sometimes a verb.

Add more examples. (Look in a dictionary and at the exercise opposite).

IN-		UN-	
decide	*indecisive*	*belief/believe*	*unbelievable*

Test yourself by covering one of the columns.
To help you remember the words you have seen, make sentences using them.

6*

3.2 **Word Formation: Adjectives – 2** . . . .

As in the previous exercise, you must first form an adjective from the words given. Next, you must form the opposite of the adjective by using **dis-, il-, im-, non-,** or **-less**. Finally, you must complete each sentence by using a suitable negative adjective. Use each form once only.

	ADJECTIVE	OPPOSITE		ADJECTIVE	OPPOSITE
alcohol	....	....	**organise**	....	....
harm	....	....	**pain**	....	....
honesty	....	....	**patience**	....	....
logic	....	....	**tact**	....	....
obey	....	....	**violence**	....	....

1. My dog won't hurt you. He's quite ....

2. He's so .... that he'd even steal from his own mother!

3. The operation will be quite .... You won't feel a thing.

4. The show was so .... that nobody knew who was coming on next.

5. We're in favour of some form of .... protest, such as occupying a building.

6. That was a rather .... remark you made about him losing all his hair!

7. I always drink something .... if I'm driving.

8. It isn't surprising if some children are .... in class if there's so little discipline at home.

9. His reasoning is totally .... I can't follow it at all.

10. Don't be so .... ! I'm sure they'll be here soon!

DIS-, IL-, IM-, NON- OR -LESS?

Put the adjectives from the exercise and the antonyms of the words below into the appropriate column. Add your own examples.
Where possible, write a 'root word' before each adjective.

agreeable	legal	mature	satisfied
careful	legible	probable	thoughtful
existent	loyal	reputable	useful

DIS-   **IL-**

agree   *disagreeable*   ....

....

....

....

                                                          IM-

....

....

....

....

        -LESS   ....

....

....

....   **NON-**

....

....

3.3 **Word Formation – Adverbs** . . . .

It is important to realise what kind of word is needed to complete the sentence in a word-transformation exercise.

In each of the sentences below you need to fill in the blank with an adverb. Sometimes a negative form will be required.

As you do the exercise, notice how the adverbs are formed and how they are used in a sentence.

Complete each sentence with the correct form of the word in brackets.

---

1. She spoke .... fast.   (INCREDIBLE)

2. It rained .... all night.   (HEAVY)

3. Could you .... help me to move these indoors?   (POSSIBLE)

4. Sales have increased .... since we started advertising our products on television.   (DRAMA)

5. She answered him .... in her quiet little voice, never once looking up at him.   (SHY)

6. Must you eat so .... ? We're trying to have a conversation!   (NOISY)

7. I'm afraid she's been .... detained.   (AVOID)

8. ...., I gave her all the help I could.   (NATURE)

9. He really upset me by speaking so .... about my idea.   (SARCASM)

10. Write .... so that the examiner can read it.   (LEGIBLE)

11. ...., I have no idea where she is, so I'm afraid I can't help you.   (FORTUNE)

12. Flooding is .... rare in this part of the world.   (COMPARE)

13. ...., I agree with the plan. It's just some of the details that I'm not so sure about.   (BASE)

14. I've been .... informed that the government intend to raise the tax on petrol.   (RELY)

15. He was .... dressed in an old brown overcoat and shoes with holes in them.   (SHABBY)

USE OF ADVERBS

Adverbs are used to modify (add to the meaning of):

- verbs   They walked **slowly** down the road.
- adjectives   She felt **extremely** tired.
- adverbs   He's eating **terribly** slowly.
- phrases   We met him **entirely** by accident.
- sentences   **Fortunately,** we had enough milk left for breakfast.

Look through the sentences on the previous page and decide what the adverb is modifying in each case.

FORMATION OF ADVERBS

Most adverbs are formed by adding **-ly** to the adjective:

	careful	**carefully**	extreme	**extremely**
but notice	full	**fully**	true	**truly**

There are a few spelling problems. (Add your own examples):

-le	comfortable	**comfortably**	possible	**possibly**

-y	easy	**easily**	happy	**happily**
but notice	shy	**shyly**		

-ic	dramatic	**dramatically**	systematic	**systematically**
but notice	public	**publicly**		

> **STUDY TIP**   In the examination you will not always be given the adjective as the word to transform. To form **truly** you may, for example, be given **truth**.
>
> This means you need to learn **all** the forms of a word.

3.4 **Word Formation – Prefixes** . . . .

Put one of the following prefixes **dis, en, mis** or **un** in front of each of the words in the list below to form verbs. Next, use the verbs you have formed to complete the sentences. Use each verb once only **in its correct form**.

..........appear	..........inform	..........lock	..........sure
..........approve	..........large	..........judge	..........understand
..........behave	..........load	..........obey	..........wrap

1. I'm afraid you've been .... We never give discounts.

2. By .... the photo we were able to read the words on the note.

3. The porter .... the door and let me in.

4. If those children .... once more, they'll go straight to bed!

5. Unfortunately, my father .... of my new girlfriend.

6. The money can't just have .... ! Somebody has stolen it!

7. After they've .... the furniture from the lorry, I'll make them a nice cup of tea.

8. I spoke very slowly and clearly so that nobody would .... what I was saying.

9. The soldier was put in prison for a week for .... orders.

10. We all gathered round to watch as she .... the parcel.

11. I .... the width of the stream and fell into the water.

12. You must always .... that the car's brakes are on properly before you start working on it.

DIS-, MIS-, EN- or UN-?

Put the verbs from the exercise into the appropriate list below.
Next use the prefixes with the words below and put them into the correct list. Some verbs can have more than one prefix.

able	**courage**	**interpret**	**pack**	**screw**
connect	**credit**	**lead**	**qualify**	**trust**

If you meet any more verbs with these prefixes, add them to your lists.

DIS-		MIS-	
....	....	....	....
....	....	....	....
....	....	....	....
....	....	....	....
....	....	....	....
....	....	....	....
....	....	....	....

UN-		EN-	OTHER PREFIXES
....	....	....	....
....	....	....	....
....	....	....	....
....	....	....	....
....	....	....	....

STUDY TIP   If there are any verbs you find difficult, write a sentence with them in. If you need help, a good dictionary should contain such sentences.

3.5 **Word Families – 1** . . . .

Complete each sentence with the correct form of the word given at the end. As you do the exercise, think about the kind of word that is needed in the sentence – verb, noun or adjective.
Be careful, because in some cases you will need a negative form.

---

1. There was .... all over the floor after he cut himself shaving. **BLEED**

2. She became more and more .... as time went by. **ANXIETY**

3. She looked at him in .... when he told her the terrible news. **BELIEVE**

4. We have still received no .... of our booking. **CONFIRM**

5. He seemed very reluctant to take my .... **ADVISE**

6. We can only catch criminals if we have the full .... of the general public. **COOPERATE**

7. She gave me a very .... look when she saw that I wasn't wearing the correct uniform. **APPROVE**

8. In ...., I would like to thank everybody who has helped to make the show such a success. **CONCLUDE**

9. She has made an invaluable .... to our efforts. **CONTRIBUTE**

10. The shop .... seemed to spend most of the time talking rather than attending to customers. **ASSIST**

11. They keep making .... statements so we don't really know what they're going to do. **CONTRADICT**

12. He's normally very .... so you'll be lucky if you get any information out of him. **COMMUNICATE**

13. He left me with no .... but to disqualify him. **CHOOSE**

14. With her .... mind she was able to work out the best way to get everybody to the meeting on time. **ANALYSE**

Below you will see a list of words relating to the exercise you have just done. Fill each blank with the correct form. If no word exists, there is a (——) in the table.

VERB	ADJECTIVE	NOUN
1.	(in)advisable advisory	adviser/advisor ....
2. analyse	....	....
3. ——	anxious	....
4. (dis)approve	(dis)	(dis) ....
5. assist	——	.... assistance
6. (dis)believe	(un)	non-believer (dis) ....
7. bleed	....	....
8.	choosy	....
9. communicate	(un) .... communicable	....
10. conclude	(in)	....
11. confirm	(un)	....
12. contradict	....	....
13. contribute	....	....
14. cooperate (co-operate)	(un)	.... cooperative

3.6 **Word Families – 2** . . . .

Complete each sentence with the correct form of the word given at the end.

1. How dare she .... us when she sits around doing nothing all day!   CRITIC

2. The mystery .... as yet another body was discovered.   DEEP

3. Everywhere you could see evidence of the .... force of the enemy bombs.   DESTROY

4. He was most .... that we should bring warm clothes.   INSIST

5. Because of her .... eyesight she's unable to paint any more pictures.   FAIL

6. That is supposed to be the .... price but you always seem to end up paying extra for something.   INCLUDE

7. We hope to see more .... schools where children of different races can get used to working together.   INTEGRATE

8. Two of the .... showed us how to do a hip throw.   INSTRUCT

9. The .... in population has led to problems in providing services such as housing and hospitals.   GROW

10. I can't stand .... so I didn't go to the top of the tower with the others.   HIGH

11. Our .... was delayed due to technical problems.   FLY

12. Every evening you hear the .... noise of motor-cycles revving up in the town square.   DEAF

13. One of the .... sat down in front of the lorry and refused to move.   DEMONSTRATE

14. It is an .... fact that children watch too much TV.   DENY

As you look these words up in your dictionary, remember to note what other forms of the word there are for you to learn.

Below you will see a list of words relating to the exercise you have just done. Fill each blank with the correct form.

VERB	ADJECTIVE	NOUN
1. criticise/ize	(un)	critic ....
2.	deaf	deafness
3. demonstrate	demonstrable (un)	....
4. deny	(un)	....
5.	....	depth
6.	.... indestructible	destruction
7. fail	....	....
8.	....	flier/flyer ....
9.	growing	grower ....
10.	high	height(s)
11.	....	inclusion
12. insist	....	....
13. integrate	.... integral	....
14. instruct	....	....

3.7 **Word Families – 3** . . . .

Complete each sentence with the correct form of the word given at the end.

1. It was an extremely .... experience, which I never want to go through again.

   PLEASE

2. The table is two metres in ....

   LONG

3. The weather is so .... that I don't know if I should take an umbrella or sun-tan lotion.

   PREDICT

4. What a .... it is to be able to put your feet up!

   RELIEVE

5. The telephone service was very .... and we spent hours trying to make a single call.

   RELY

6. The sea defences need to be .... before the winter to reduce the risk of flooding.

   STRONG

7. There's a .... of highly-skilled engineers so we might have difficulty getting the work done.

   SHORT

8. She's not really .... for this job as she hasn't had the right sort of training.

   SUIT

9. As her only .... relative, he expects to inherit all her money.

   SURVIVE

10. If they .... the road, that will mean more traffic and maybe more pedestrians being knocked over.

    WIDE

11. His .... to sponsor the event came as a great shock.

    REFUSE

12. I wish I shared his ...., but I really don't think this will work.

    OPTIMIST

13. I could only get tickets for the afternoon ....

    PERFORM

14. They're very .... about our chances of success.

    PESSIMISM

Below you will see a list of words relating to the exercise you have just done. Fill each blank with the correct form.

VERB	ADJECTIVE	NOUN
1.	.... lengthy	length
2. ——	....	optimist ....
3.	performing	performer ....
4. ——	....	.... pessimism
5. (dis)please	(un)	(dis) ....
6. predict	(un)	.... (un)predictability
7. refuse	——	....
8.	(un)relieved	....
9.	(un)	(un)reliability reliance
10.	short	.... shortness
11.	....	strength
12.	(un)	(un)suitability
13. survive	....	.... survival
14.	....	width

3.8 **Word Families – 4** . . . .

Complete each sentence with the correct form of the word given at the end.

---

1. Some of the .... in this dictionary are more difficult to understand than the word they're explaining.   DEFINE

2. He'll be away for an .... period.   DEFINE

3. We have to .... on electricity so make sure you switch off all the lights when you leave.   ECONOMY

4. All the leading .... say that this country is heading for a recession.   ECONOMY

5. We're .... twins so people have great difficulty telling us apart. IDENTITY

6. You'll need some form of .... if you want to draw money out of your account.   IDENTIFY

7. This is just an .... of the kind of thing that could happen if you don't wear a seat belt.   ILLUSTRATE

8. The judges were especially impressed by the .... use of light and shade in the painting.   IMAGINE

9. I was not very .... by his so-called comedy act.   IMPRESS

10. She is at a very .... age so we must make sure that she goes around with the right sort of people.   IMPRESS

11. It was supposed to be a .... performance but you could see she was miming.   LIFE

12. I consider him to be one of our greatest .... poets.   LIFE

13. This is the site of the .... extension to the motorway.   PROPOSE

14. After my holiday I had to get back to the .... of the daily office routine.   REAL

15. There are .... ways of making this soup but I think mine is the best. VARY

16. I've led a full and .... life but now I feel it's time to settle down. VARY

Below you will see a list of words relating to the exercise you have just done. Fill each blank with the correct form.

VERB	ADJECTIVE	NOUN
1.	(un)defined indefinable definitive (in)	....
2.	(un) .... (un)economical	.... economics
3.	(un) .... (un)identifiable	identity ....
4. illustrate	.... illustrative	....
5. imagine	(un)imaginable .... (un)imaginative	....
6. impress	(un)impressed .... (un)	impression
7. live	.... live .... living	.... living livelihood
8. propose	....	proposer .... proposition
9. —	real (un)	.... realist realism
10.	.... (in)	.... variation variability

7–1215

3.9 **Word Formation**. . . . . REVISION

Read the text and use the word given at the end of the line to form a word which will fill the blank.

A LENGTHY WAIT

We spent a few (1) .... days waiting until the ANXIETY
(2) .... of our holiday finally came through. We were CONFIRM
not exactly (3) .... by the efficiency of what we had IMPRESS
been told was a (4) .... travel company. REPUTATION

My mother was most (5) .... that I should phone her as INSIST
soon as we arrived in New York. Rather (6) .... I had OPTIMISM
assured her that we would (7) .... be there by six at the DEFINE
latest.

(8) ...., when we all arrived at the airport, we found FORTUNE
that our (9) .... had been delayed. When he heard this, FLY
John, our youngest, showed his (10) .... by lying on the PLEASE
floor and sulking. I soon lost (11) .... with him after my PATIENT
attempts to bribe him with an ice cream and sweets proved completely
(12) .... SUCCEED

We had no (13) .... but to settle down in a departure CHOOSE
lounge full of (14) .... children. You can imagine my NOISE
(15) .... when we were finally called to board the plane. RELIEVE

(16) .... , I thought that our troubles would now be over. NATURE
I was wrong. John made it clear that it was (17) .... REAL
of us to expect him to walk all the way to the boarding gate.
All his energy had mysteriously (18) .... We tried APPEAR
gentle persuasion, sweets, and more promises of ice cream, but they
were all (19) .... I had to carry him along the endless USE
corridors and just as my (20) .... was about to give out, STRONG
I saw the gate number in front of me. It was number 13!

CONFUSING WORDS

4

In the first part of Paper 3 (Use of English) you have to differentiate between words and phrases which you might find confusing.

Look at the following example:

> We expect ten more people .... Mary.
> **A** beside   **B** besides   **C** in addition   **D** otherwise

The correct answer is **besides**.

The word **beside** has a similar spelling but has the meaning **next to**:
> Come and sit **beside** me.

The phrase **in addition** must be followed by **to**:
> We expect ten more people **in addition to** Mary.

The word **otherwise** is not used in front of a noun in this way but to join two parts of a sentence like this:
> I must leave now, **otherwise** I'll miss my bus.

When you meet any words or phrases that you find confusing, it is important to note them down and make sure you know how to use them **in a sentence.**

4.1 **Confusing Words – 1** . . . .

Complete each sentence by using a suitable word from the list.
You may find that some of the words can be used in more than one sentence but you must use each of the words once only.

EXERCISE 1   apologetic   apologise   apology   excuse   **forgive**   **regret**   **sorry**

---

1. I really must .... for making such a mess.

2. They .... not telling him earlier.

3. There's no .... for this type of behaviour.

4. She's .... she wasn't able to help you more.

5. I can never .... them for all the trouble they've caused.

6. He was most .... about the delay.

7. I hope he'll accept my .... so that we can be friends again.

EXERCISE 2   **advice**   **advise**   **insist**   **make**   **persuade**   **suggest**

---

1. In the end they managed to .... him to take another route.

2. Do you think I could offer you some .... ?

3. I would .... you not to delay any longer.

4. You must always .... on seeing the manager.

5. We can't .... you come with us, of course.

6. I would .... setting out early in the morning.

EXERCISE 3   **although**   **despite**   **however**   **in spite**   **though**

---

1. .... hard he tried, he still couldn't open the door.

2. Even .... he was reluctant at first, he joined in the fun.

3. .... her illness, she decided to go to the concert.

4. .... he wasn't keen on the idea, he agreed to go.

5. I managed to arrive on time .... of the chaos on the roads.

Write two sentences of your own, one above and one below the line, to show that you understand the differences between the words.
Use the blanks to do the same for other word contrasts that you want to remember from the exercise opposite or any others you find.

1. **ALTHOUGH** / **DESPITE** ....

2. **ADVICE** / **ADVISE** ....

3. **BRING** / **TAKE** ....

4. **NOTE** / **NOTICE** ....

5. **BORROW** / **LEND** ....

6. **RAISE** / **RISE** ....

7. ( ) ....

8. ( ) ....

9. ( ) ....

Check from time to time by covering the example sentences to see if you can remember the difference.

4.2 **Confusing Words – 2** . . . .

Complete each sentence by using a word or phrase from the list. Use each word once only.

EXERCISE 1   accustomed   apparent   aware   familiar   sense   sensible   sensitive

---

1. Are you .... of any reason for his disappearance?

2. It's always .... to take an umbrella on cloudy days like this.

3. There was no .... reason for her bad mood.

4. I'm not .... with this machine.

5. She soon got .... to driving on the other side of the road.

6. Her skin was so .... that she used a special kind of soap.

7. There's little .... in waiting any longer.

EXERCISE 2   alike   common   identical   like   shared   similar   the same

---

1. Our jobs are different but his salary is .... as mine.

2. A pointed chin is a feature .... by many members of my family.

3. Her tastes are very .... to mine.

4. I wish I had a swimming pool .... my next-door neighbour's.

5. We are united by a .... goal – to win the competition.

6. You must treat all pupils .... and not have any favourites.

7. That handbag is .... to the one I bought last week.

EXERCISE 3   denied   disagreed   disapproved   objected   refused   rejected

---

1. They .... his plans for improving the show.

2. She .... to do as I had asked.

3. The suspect .... breaking into the house.

4. I .... with him about where to hold the meeting.

5. My parents .... of me going out with somebody his age.

6. He .... to paying extra for having breakfast in his room.

Write two sentences, one above and one below the line, to show that you understand the differences between the words.
Use the blanks to do the same for other word contrasts that you want to remember from the exercise opposite or any others you find.

1. **SENSIBLE** / **SENSITIVE** ....

2. **IDENTICAL** / **THE SAME** ....

3. **HARD** / **HARDLY** ....

4. **FIT** / **SUIT** ....

5. **CONVENIENT** / **SUITABLE** ....

6. **MENTION** / **REFER** ....

7. ....

8. ....

9. ....

Check from time to time by covering the example sentences to see if you can remember the difference.

4.3 **Confusing Words – 3** . . . .

Complete each sentence by using a word from the list. Use each word once only.

EXERCISE 1 **apart** **beside** **besides** **except** **instead** **only** **otherwise**

---

1. .... Selena decided not to take part.

2. Everybody's here .... for Lois.

3. Clark is the boy sitting .... Lana.

4. .... from Bruce, is there anyone else who needs transport?

5. There are three other boys in the family .... Dick.

6. .... of answering, she just stared into space.

7. I need the car myself, ... I'd let you borrow it.

EXERCISE 2 **avoid** **divert** **guard** **prevent** **protect**

---

1. You wear a helmet to .... yourself against falling stones.

2. They tried to .... him from seeing their daughter.

3. We need more men to .... the prisoners.

4. They had to .... the traffic down side streets.

5. She went a different way to .... meeting him again.

EXERCISE 3 **capable** **fit** **manage** **possible** **skilled** **succeed** **successful**

---

1. I wasn't very .... in persuading him to change his plans.

2. You're not .... to drive in that condition!

3. It wasn't .... to get an appointment before Friday morning.

4. They didn't .... in waking anybody up.

5. He wasn't .... of understanding how to work the machine.

6. Did you .... to get tickets for tonight's match?

7. We need some more .... workers in the engineering department.

Write two sentences, one above and one below the line, to show that you understand the differences between the words.
Use the blanks to do the same for other word contrasts that you want to remember from the exercise opposite or any others you find.

1. (**AVOID** / **PREVENT**) ....

2. (**MANAGE** / **SUCCEED**) ....

3. (**CHECK** / **CONTROL**) ....

4. (**LACK** / **FAILURE**) ....

5. (**DISMISS** / **RESIGN**) ....

6. (**REMEMBER** / **REMIND**) ....

7. (..........) ....

8. (..........) ....

9 (..........) ....

Check from time to time by covering the example sentences to see if you can remember the difference.

4.4 **Confusing Words – 4** . . . .

Complete each sentence by using a word from the list. Use each word once only.

EXERCISE 1 appeal   fancy   fascinated   fond   glad   interested   keen

---

1. I'm not very .... on this new chocolate bar.

2. They were .... by the way the animals stored their food.

3. How long have you been .... in collecting stamps?

4. The idea of working abroad should .... to him.

5. I'm really .... of chocolate with nuts in it.

6. Do you .... going for a swim this evening?

7. I'd be .... to help if they really wanted me to.

EXERCISE 2 accused arrested blamed charged complained condemned protested sentenced

---

1. In her speech she .... the use of unnecessary violence.

2. Many guests .... about the lack of adequate heating.

3. He was .... of stealing the necklace.

4. He will be .... with murdering his nephew.

5. She .... her brother for losing the family fortune.

6. The police have .... her for drunken driving.

7. The judge .... them to 2 years' imprisonment.

8. The demonstrators .... against the new motorway.

EXERCISE 3 agree   allow   let   permission   permit

---

1. You need a special .... before you can work in this country.

2. She gave me .... to use the hall this evening.

3. I don't think they'll .... you try that again!

4. How could they .... so many people into the stadium?

5. Will she .... to their request?

Write two sentences, one above and one below the line, to show that you understand the differences between the words.

Use the blanks to do the same for other word contrasts that you want to remember from the exercise opposite or any others you find.

1. **FOND / KEEN** ....

2. **ALLOW / LET** ....

3. **ANNOUNCE / INFORM** ....

4. **PRIZE / REWARD** ....

5. **DIRECTION / DIRECTIONS** ....

6. **WAY / PATH** ....

7. ....

8. ....

9. ....

Check from time to time by covering the example sentences to see if you can remember the difference.

4.5 **Confusing Words** . . . . REVISION

Look at the set of four alternatives given at the bottom of the page and choose the one which fills the blank.

My secretary (1) .... me that I had an important meeting that evening. She (2) .... me not to set off too late, (3) .... I might get held up in the rush hour traffic.

I asked my boss for (4) .... to leave work early so that I could (5) .... the traffic jams. He was not very (6) .... on the idea at first, but eventually I was able to (7) .... him to (8) .... me go at 4.30 (9) .... 5 o'clock. Even (10) .... this was not as early as I had hoped, it was better than nothing.

I had (11) .... started on my journey when I found that there had been a major accident on my route. All the traffic was (12) .... down some side streets and I found myself in a part of town that I wasn't (13) .... with. I asked a passer-by for (14) .... and I finally (15) .... to get back to the main road. As I was now late, I drove rather too fast and was (16) .... by the police for speeding. I never got to my meeting.

1.	A	announced	B	remembered	C	reminded	D	said
2.	A	advised	B	guarded	C	insisted	D	suggested
3.	A	beside	B	besides	C	except	D	otherwise
4.	A	allowance	B	permission	C	permit	D	possibility
5.	A	avoid	B	deny	C	prevent	D	reject
6.	A	fond	B	glad	C	happy	D	keen
7.	A	advice	B	agree	C	make	D	persuade
8.	A	allow	B	get	C	let	D	permit
9.	A	apart from	B	except for	C	in spite of	D	instead of
10.	A	although	B	however	C	though	D	whether
11.	A	hard	B	hardly	C	justly	D	sooner
12.	A	diversion	B	diverted	C	prevented	D	rejected
13.	A	accustomed	B	apparent	C	familiar	D	sensible
14.	A	direction	B	directions	C	path	D	way
15.	A	managed	B	succeeded	C	was capable	D	was successful
16.	A	accused	B	arrested	C	blamed	D	charged

GRAMMAR REVISION

5

In everything you write and say during the different parts of the examination, you should pay particular attention to your grammar. Throughout your course, your teacher will help you to revise all the most important points of English grammar.

In this special revision section, you can work on 8 of the most important points which are most often tested in Paper 3 (Use of English).

Comparison	**The Present Perfect**
So and such	**Reported Speech**
The -ing form	**Conditionals**
The Infinitive	**The Passive**

If you have difficulty with any one of these points, pay special attention to it.

In each unit there are exercises which are similar to the examination questions. However, it is important to **think** about these grammar points to see which patterns you have to learn.

On the right-hand page of each unit you will find a summary of each of these points. This will help you to think about them more clearly just before the examination.

It is very important to write some examples of your own in each of these sections. In particular, think of sentences which might be useful to you in your Speaking exam – sentences which are true for your life and experience.

5.1 **Comparison** . . . .

Complete the following so that the meaning of each sentence is similar:

1. a. Ivan is a better tennis player than me.

   b. Ivan plays tennis .... me.

   c. I don't play tennis .... Ivan does.

2. a. My brother is .... I am.

   b. My brother drives more carefully than me.

   c. I don't drive .... my brother.

For a summary of the rules, see opposite.

EXERCISE 2   Use the word given and other words to complete the second sentence so that it means the same as the first one. You must use between two and five words, including the word given.

1. Britain isn't as warm as Greece.
   climate
   Greece .... Britain.

2. Peter eats more quickly than Diana.
   fast
   Diana doesn't .... Peter.

3. Do you sell a more powerful drill?
   powerful
   Is this... you sell?

4. Our boss works harder than anyone else in this firm.
   nobody
   In this firm .... as our boss does.

5. I've never met such a strange person.
   ever
   She is the .... met.

6. I was less interested by the film than I'd expected.
   wasn't
   The film .... I'd expected.

7. Nobody in the club plays badminton as well as she does.
   player
   She is... in the club.

COMPARISON OF ADJECTIVES

REGULAR	tall	taller	the tallest
	simple	simpler	the simplest
	comfortable	more comfortable	the most comfortable
		less comfortable	the least comfortable
	easy	easier	the easiest
Be careful of the spelling!	hot	hotter	the hottest
IRREGULAR	good	better	the best
	bad	worse	the worst

COMPARISON OF ADVERBS

REGULAR	carefully	more carefully	the most carefully
		less carefully	the least carefully
IRREGULAR	well	better	the best
	badly	worse	the worst
	fast	faster	the fastest
	hard	harder	the hardest

SIMILARITY AND DIFFERENCE

He is (not) **as** tall **as** his sister.

They (don't) speak **as** fluently **as** we do.

In the Speaking exam you may want to talk about yourself using comparatives. Fill in the spaces with information which is true for you:

YOUR COUNTRY: The most important city in my country is ....

My country is (not) .... it was 100 years ago.

YOUR TOWN: My town used to be .... than it is now.

It isn't as .... as it used to be.

YOU: I am .... than most of my friends.

My best friend is more .... than me.

5.2 **So** and **Such** . . . .

EXERCISE 1 Put **so, such** or **such a(n)** in these sentences.

---

1. I wish I wasn't .... tired all the time!

2. Miss Wilson types .... slowly. I could write faster!

3. .... few people came that the meeting was cancelled.

4. That was .... good film – I'd love to see it again.

5. They played .... old-fashioned records, I almost laughed.

6. We had .... awful weather in the North, we came home a week early.

For a summary of the rules, see opposite.

EXERCISE 2 Use the word given and other words to complete the second sentence so that it means the same as the first one. You must use between two and five words, including the word given.

---

1. The opening wasn't large enough for the dog to get through.
    small
    The opening .... that the dog couldn't get through.

2. It was so noisy that we walked out.
    much
    There was .... that we walked out.

3. The coffee was too strong for us to drink.
    such
    It was .... couldn't drink it.

4. If he didn't have such bad writing, I could read his letters.
    badly
    He .... that I can't read his letters.

5. It was the most beautiful view I'd ever seen.
    never
    I .... beautiful view before.

6. If he had driven faster, he wouldn't have annoyed everybody.
    slowly
    He .... that he annoyed everybody.

7. They didn't give us enough time to do the job properly.
    little
    We were given .... couldn't do the job properly.

GRAMMAR SUMMARY

Write the correct example in the space after each rule.

| such high prices | so cold | such a shame |
| such loud music | so quietly | so much money |

1. **SO**   + an adjective   ....
2. **SO**   + an adverb   ....
3. **SO**   + few, many, much, little   ....
4. **SUCH A(N)** + a singular countable noun   ....
5. **SUCH**   + a plural noun   ....
6. **SUCH**   + an uncountable noun   ....

Now organise the following words and phrases:

lovely weather	quickly	difficult question	many people
fresh bread	warm bed	awful children	pleasant music
loud bang	much time	terrible storms	high mountains
clothes	few ideas	heavy rain	angry
violent	carelessly	little time	dark
historic city	cheap	deeply	dangerously

1. SO + adjective

....

....

....

....

2. SO + adverb

....

....

....

....

3. SO + few etc

....

....

....

....

4. SUCH A(N) + singular

....

....

....

....

5. SUCH + plural

....

....

....

....

6. SUCH + uncountable

....

....

....

....

5.3 **The -ing form** . . . .

Use the word given and other words to complete the second sentence so that it means the same as the first one. You must use between two and five words, including the word given.

---

1. Don't stay out in the sun too long.
avoid
You should .... in the sun too long.

2. It was very difficult for me to understand your writing.
difficulty
I had .... your writing.

3. Her father wouldn't let me speak to her.
prevented
Her father .... to her.

4. Bill said he was sorry he was late.
apologised
Bill .... late.

5. "You broke my bracelet, Sophie!" said Anne.
accused
Anne .... bracelet.

6. I don't like playing squash very much.
keen
I'm not very .... squash.

7. You won't get anywhere if you shout at him.
use
It's no .... at him.

8. Chris didn't play tennis but went swimming instead.
instead
Chris went swimming .... tennis.

9. She doesn't want to get up early.
objects
She .... early.

10. Please don't repeat everything I say.
mind
Would .... everything I say.

11. He'd rather watch TV than go out to the cinema.
prefers
He .... to going out to the cinema.

12. This is the first time I've driven this type of car.
used
I'm not .... this type of car.

Below you will see examples of the ways in which the **-ing** form is used.
Add your own examples to the lists. (See the opposite page.)

PREPOSITION + -ing

before starting ....

....

....

ADJECTIVE + PREPOSITION + -ing

good at swimming ....

....

....

VERB + -ing

dislike being interrupted ....

....

....

VERB + PREPOSITION +-ing

apologise for coming late ....

....

....

Now write sentences about yourself:

I'm looking forward to ....

I sometimes have difficulty ....

I spent yesterday evening ....

I'm not used to ....

I really hate ....

8*

5.4 **The Infinitive** . . . .

Use the word given and other words to complete the second sentence so that it means the same as the first one. You must use between two and five words, including the word given.

1. He's too young to see the film.
    enough
    He isn't .... to see the film.

2. "If I were you, Kate, I'd wear a different pair of shoes."
    advised
    He .... a different pair of shoes.

3. I'd rather you came at six o'clock.
    prefer
    I .... come at six o'clock.

4. Older people often have difficulty finding a job.
    difficult
    It's often .... find a job.

5. They say he's living in Vancouver.
    said
    He .... in Vancouver.

6. Why did you allow them to leave early yesterday?
    let
    You shouldn't .... early yesterday.

7. The explanation was so complicated that I couldn't understand it.
    too
    The explanation .... to understand.

8. I'm sorry, but I don't want to talk about it.
    rather
    I'm sorry, but .... about it.

9. "Please sing us another song, Murray."
    persuade
    They tried to .... another song.

10. I don't suppose you know where he lives, do you?
    happen
    Do .... where he lives?

11. It looks as if they left last night.
    seem
    They .... last night.

12. I advised him not to see her again.
    better
    "You .... her again."

Look at the uses of the infinitive listed below and add your own examples. (See the opposite page.)

VERB + INFINITIVE

agree to come ....

....

....

VERB +  + INFINITIVE

allow him to leave early ....

....

....

....

ADJECTIVE + INFINITIVE

easy to see ....

....

....

Now make sentences of your own:

One day I hope to ....

Some parents don't let ....

It's difficult for me ....

I wish I had enough money ....

British people are said ....

The weather seems ....

5.5 **The Present Perfect** . . . .

EXERCISE 1   Put the verbs in brackets into the present perfect. Some verbs may need the continuous form.

---

1. They .... (TRY) to understand these instructions for half an hour and they're still not getting anywhere!

2. I'm nervous because I .... (NEVER DRIVE) on the motorway before.

3. I can't find my watch. I'm sure someone .... (STEAL) it!

4. They .... (VISIT) Italy several times but this will be their first trip to Sicily.

5. I .... (STAND) here for hours, waiting for you to come.

6. This is the first time we .... (EAT) real Spanish paella.

EXERCISE 2   Use the word given and other words to complete the second sentence so that it means the same as the first one. You must use between two and five words, including the word given.

---

1. He started work here three years ago.
    working
    He .... the past three years.

2. I've never had problems with this typewriter before.
    time
    This is the .... problems with this typewriter.

3. She last saw him when she was ten.
    seen
    She .... she was ten.

4. It will be my fourth visit to Athens.
    been
    I .... times so far.

5. I've never been so happy.
    happier
    I'm .... been in my whole life.

6. This room is still in a mess.
    tidied
    This room .... yet.

7. They last ate three days ago.
    anything
    They .... three days.

GRAMMAR SUMMARY

The present perfect is a **present** tense. It is used to **look back from now** on an action or period of time, for example:

I'**ve been waiting** here for almost an hour.
She'**s visited** Greece many times but she'**s never been** to Corinth.
I'**ve never eaten** such terrible food.
This is the most terrible food I'**ve ever eaten.**

Often, we see the **result** of an action and talk of its cause, for example:

Think: I can't find my wallet anywhere.
Say: My wallet **has been stolen.**

Think: I'm a little nervous.
Say: **I've never flown** before.

You do **not** use the present perfect when you are talking about a specific time in the past:

I've been to New York three times. I last **went** there two years ago.

I've just read an article about ways of making money. It **was** fascinating.

In the interview you may have to use the present perfect to talk about yourself. Write answers to these questions:

1. **Have you ever been abroad?**

    ....
    (If the answer is "Yes", say which countries you've been to.)

2. **How long have you been living in your town/city/village?**

    ....

3. **Have you ever read any books in English?**

    ....
    (If the answer is "Yes", say which books you have read.)

4. **What exciting/interesting things have you done in the past year?**

    ....

5. **What are your ambitions?**

    I've always wanted to ....

5.6 **Reported Speech** . . . .

Use the word given and other words to complete the second sentence so that it means the same as the first one. You must use between two and five words, including the word given.

1. "Are you having problems, Stuart?
   asked
   I .... having problems.

2. "I won't eat my vegetables!"
   refused
   She .... vegetables.

3. "This is the first time the train has been late."
   never
   We pointed out that .... late before.

4. "Please, please let me go to the disco!" she asked them.
   begged
   She .... go to the disco.

5. "Where's the meeting on Friday?"
   asked
   He .... on Friday.

6. She advised Mike to take his car.
   better
   "You .... car, Mike."

7. "I'm having my flat re-decorated."
   said
   Mary .... flat re-decorated.

8. "Don't make such a fuss, John!"
   not
   Ruth told .... such a fuss.

9. "What are they going to do?"
   know
   I wanted .... going to do.

10. "I'll come if I have time."
    offered
    Wendy .... had time.

11. "Why did they look at me in such a strange way?"
    wondered
    She .... at her in such a strange way.

12. "Why don't you try to find another job?"
    look
    She suggested to Arnold .... another job.

STATEMENTS AND QUESTIONS

When you transform a statement, you must be careful about the change in tense as well as the pronouns and possessive adjectives.

In addition, when you transform a question, you must be very careful about the word order.

Study these examples:

"I hate grammar."	He said **he hated grammar.**
"Where's your book?"	We asked her **where her book was.**
"I'm doing my homework."	She said **she was doing her homework.**
"I've finished mine"	He said **he had finished his.**
"When did you finish?"	She asked him **when he had finished.**
"We can't do any more."	They said **they couldn't do any more.**

Remember that you might not have **say** or **ask** at the beginning of your sentence. Look back at the exercise on the opposite page and see what other verbs can be used.

OTHER REPORTED SPEECH CONSTRUCTIONS

Study these examples:

"Come with me."	He **asked/told/begged** her to come with him.
"Don't interrupt"	She **warned/ordered** me not to interrupt.
"We'll help you."	They **offered/promised/agreed** to help her.
"I won't do it!"	He **refused** to do it.
"Why don't you wait?"	She **advised** him to wait.
	She **suggested** that he should wait.

Now complete these sentences about yourself, using a reported speech construction:

1. **When I was very young my parents told me** ....

   ....

2. **I remember that one day my teacher asked me** ....

   ....

3. **The other day my friend wanted to know** ....

   ....

5.7 **Conditionals** . . . .

EXERCISE 1   Put the verb in brackets into the correct form.

---

1. I'll only go if he .... (APOLOGISE).

2. If she .... (KNOW) he was going to be so angry about it, she wouldn't have done it.

3. She'll have to fire him unless his work .... (IMPROVE).

4. If we hadn't missed the train, we .... (ARRIVE) on time.

5. If I knew where they were, I .... (TAKE) you there now.

6. You wouldn't be so tired today if you .... (GO) to bed when I told you to.

EXERCISE 2   Use the word given and other words to complete the second sentence so that it means the same as the first one. You must use between two and five words, including the word given.

---

1. We couldn't afford to buy the car.
   enough
   If we .... we would have bought the car.

2. You won't pass if you don't revise more.
   unless
   You won't pass .... more.

3. It was only because of her help that I managed to do it.
   never
   If she hadn't helped .... managed to do it.

4. He was driving too fast so he crashed.
   so
   If he .... fast he wouldn't have crashed.

5. You feel tired all the time because you go to bed so late.
   earlier
   If you .... you wouldn't feel tired all the time.

6. She'll leave unless he arrives in the next ten minutes.
   if
   She'll leave .... in the next ten minutes.

7. Oh why did I eat that pie last night!
   wish
   I .... that pie last night!

GRAMMAR SUMMARY

The forms which you are most likely to meet in the exam are:

1. **'ll (will)**			**present simple**
She'll have to go	**if**		they phone her.
I won't leave	**unless**		he comes.

2. **'d (would)**			**past simple**
I'd buy a new car	**if**		I had enough money.
You wouldn't cough so much			you didn't smoke.

3. **'d (would) have**			**past perfect**
I would have understood	**if**		he had spoken more slowly.
You wouldn't have crashed			you had been concentrating.

Sometimes you may have a combination such as:

4. **'d (would)**			**past perfect**
I'd still have a job today	**if**		I hadn't been rude to my boss.
He wouldn't feel so ill			he hadn't eaten so much.

In Question 3, Paper 3 (Use of English) you may also have to use the following structures, with the same tenses as those you have just seen:

5. **present simple**   **'ll (will)**
In case it's cold,   I'll take my overcoat.

6.   **past**
I wish | I had enough money, then I'd buy a car.
If only |

7.   **past perfect**
I wish | he had spoken more slowly, then I would have understood.
If only |

Now write sentences about yourself:

If I had enough money, ...

I wish ....

If I had to live somewhere else, ...

If I hadn't ....

5.8 **The Passive** . . . .

EXERCISE 1   Put the following passive forms into the sentences:

is made   **is being made**   **was made**   **has been made**   **will be made**   **had been made**

---

1. Cheese .... from milk.

2. The pen I lost .... in Hong Kong.

3. The decision .... at this very moment.

4. They were allowed to return after the bomb .... safe.

5. This blue cheese .... locally for a very long time.

6. In future all private calls .... from the new pay phone.

EXERCISE 2   Use the word given and other words to complete the second sentence so that it means the same as the first one. You must use between two and five words, including the word given.

---

1. You can't get into the park after 10 pm every night.
    closed
    The gates .... at 10 pm every night.

2. This table is still dirty.
    cleaned
    This table .... yet.

3. They're interviewing her at the moment.
    interviewed
    She .... at the moment.

4. They'd just sold the last ticket.
    bought
    The last ticket .... someone else.

5. The jury will decide tomorrow.
    made
    The .... the jury tomorrow.

6. I can't believe that nobody saw him.
    must
    Surely he .... somebody.

7. Take these pills twice a day.
    must
    These pills .... twice a day.

GRAMMAR SUMMARY

Look at these two sentences. The 'normal' active form is no. 1, but in a newspaper you may read the passive form – no. 2.

1. Jones scored the winning goal.

2. The winning goal was scored by Jones.

In English, the first words of a sentence are usually what the sentence is about – the topic. The new information is given later in the sentence.

1. is a sentence about Jones - so he comes first.

2. is a sentence about the winning goal - so it comes first.

The passive is formed from part of the verb **be** + the past participle. Study these examples and think about other sentences you could make:

Over 100 bicycles **are stolen** every week.
The programme **is being recorded** at the moment.
This house **was built** 20 years ago.
Some improvements **have been made** since we last looked at it.
I realised that my car **had been taken away** by the police.
This medicine will/should/must **be taken** at regular intervals.

In the Speaking exam you may need the passive to talk about yourself. Here are some common situations where it is natural. Write sentences in the passive which are true for you:

1. I was born in .... **in** ....
              (place)   (year)

2. My favourite book is .... **It was written by** ....
                       (title)   (author)

3. My favourite record is .... **It was recorded by** ....
                        (title)   (singer/group)

4. One of the oldest buildings in my town is the .... **I think it was built around**

    ....
    (year)

5. An important new facility in my town is the ....

    It was ....

This exercise is like Question 3 of Paper 3 (Use of English).
Use the word given and other words to complete the second sentence so that it means the same as the first one. You must use between two and five words, including the word given.

1. "Why didn't you come on time?"
   I
   She asked .... come on time.

2. She's a better tennis player than I am.
   well
   I don't .... she does.

3. They think he travelled there by train.
   believed
   He is .... there by train.

4. He drove so badly that he kept having accidents.
   driver
   He was .... that he kept having accidents.

5. "Would you mind not watching me all the time, Sarah?"
   objected
   Andy .... all the time.

6. Really, I would prefer to come tomorrow.
   rather
   Really, ... tomorrow.

7. Why didn't I ask her out?
   only
   If .... her out!

8. The council decided yesterday.
   made
   The .... the council yesterday.

9. "Which room is it in?"
   wondered
   She .... in.

10. I've never met such a strong man.
    ever
    He's the .... met.

11. If the bread hadn't been so stale we would have eaten it.
    too
    The bread was .... to eat.

12. This is the first time I've written this kind of letter.
    used
    I'm not .... this kind of letter.

COMMON MISTAKES

6

As you try to speak and write English, you will make mistakes. This is normal, and nothing to worry about. It's all part of the learning process.

You should get worried, however, if you keep on making the same mistakes. You need to understand what you've done wrong and make sure you get it right the next time.

This section is designed to make you aware of your mistakes. The more aware you are, the fewer mistakes you will make.

The first two units present you with mistakes which are very common for students all over the world. With each mistake you are given a clue to what is wrong, for example:

> *I have seen him yesterday.*
> Use a past tense if you mention a time in the past.

You must then write the correct sentence on the right-hand page:

> *I saw him yesterday.*

There are two extra units for you to make notes about your own mistakes.

You will need to check with your teacher that you have written correct English. Near the exam, cover the right-hand page, and check all the mistakes again. You want to avoid them in the exam!

Each of these sentences contains a mistake. Look at the notes underneath. Mark the part which is wrong with a coloured pen. Write the correct sentence in the box on the next page.

---

1. *Top tennis players are not smoking.*

Use the Present Simple for things which are general.

2. *I live in the Belmont Road.*

Do not use *the* with street names.

3. *The team didn't play as good as I had expected.*

Good is an **adjective** ; *well* is the **adverb** .

4. *The news are so depressing at the moment.*

Some singulars look plural, eg *mathematics, billiards, measles.*

5. *They asked him where was the police station.*

Word order in reported speech!

6. *Is he coming too?—I don't hope so.*

I hope so; I hope not; but *I think so; I don't think so.*

7. *I can't afford a holiday. I don't have money enough.*

Enough comes **after** an adjective but **before** a noun.

8. *Go Cromwell Street along.*

Prepositions come before.

9. *Have you got an own room?*

I can have *my own room* or *a room of my own* .

10. *We had a so good time.*

So + adjective; *such (a)* + adjective followed by a noun. (See 5.2)

11. *In my country we start the school when we are six.*

Do not use *the* if you mean 'school in general.'

12. *They have 4 children which are very amusing.*

Who with people, *which* with things.

Write the correct sentences in the boxes.
When you revise for the exam, cover this page, and try to remember what the correct sentence is before checking.

1.
2.
3.
4.
5.
6.
7.
8.
9.
10.
11.
12.

9–1215

Each of these sentences contains a mistake. Look at the notes underneath. Mark the part which is wrong with a coloured pen. Write the correct sentence in the box on the next page.

1. *I have been living here in Spain since 2 years.*

   Since with a point in time, *for* with a period.

2. *I am living here since I was 10 years old.*

   Use the Present Perfect to look back on a period of time.

3. *She is born in 1900.*

   Use the past tense in English here.

4. *I try my best not to do mistakes.*

   Remember the difference between *do* and *make*.

5. *We have had such a terrible weather.*

   Weather is an uncountable noun.

6. *She went always to work by bus.*

   Word order!

7. *I don't can see you until the day after tomorrow.*

   Never use *don't* before modals; make the negative by adding *n't*.

8. *Yesterday was a holiday. We didn't must go to school.*

   For necessity in the past, use *have to*.

9. *I haven't never been there before.*

   You mustn't have two negatives.

10. *Are you interesting to learn this or not?*

    The theatre is *interesting*. I am *interested* in it.

11. *My sister has twenty years.*

    In English you *are … years old*.

12. *When you come tomorrow, can you take the book I lent you?*

    You *go* and *take* ; you *come* and *bring*.

Write the correct sentences in the boxes.
When you revise for the exam, cover this page, and try to remember what the correct sentence is before checking.

1.

2.

3.

4.

5.

6.

7.

8.

9.

10.

11.

12.

9*

6.3 **My Mistakes – 1** . . . .

This page is for your mistakes. If your teacher points out a serious mistake in a composition, for example, write it down here.
Make a mark to show where the mistake is and add a note underneath, as in 6.1–6.2.
Ask your teacher if you have any difficulty.
Write the correct sentence on the opposite page.

1.	*My sister live in America.*
	3rd person S! – in present simple singular
2.	
3.	
4.	
5.	
6.	
7.	
8.	
9.	
10.	
11.	
12.	

Write the correct sentences below.
Remember to check these sentences again before the exam.

1.	*My sister lives in America.*
2.	
3.	
4.	
5.	
6.	
7.	
8.	
9.	
10.	
11.	
12.	

6.4 **My Mistakes – 2** . . . .

This page is for your mistakes. If your teacher points out a serious mistake in a composition, for example, write it down here.
Make a mark to show where the mistake is and add a note underneath, as in 6.1–6.2.
Ask your teacher if you have any difficulty.
Write the correct sentence on the opposite page.

1.
2.
3.
4.
5.
6.
7.
8.
9.
10.
11.
12.

Write the correct sentences below.
Remember to check these sentences again before the exam.

1.
2.
3.
4.
5.
6.
7.
8.
9.
10.
11.
12.

6.5 **Spelling** . . . . REVISION

SUMMARY

You can lose marks in the exam if you make careless spelling mistakes.

Make sure you know and can spell the following simple words that students often spell wrongly.

with	there	here	passed
which	their	hear	past
what			
when	its	read	though
while	it's	red	although
who			through
how	who's	quite	
where	whose	quiet	because

The following common words can cause spelling problems:

friend	serious	thought	making
full	beautiful	advertisement	except
whether	department	stayed	choice

Now make a list of the words which you personally have to be careful with:

....	....	....	....
....	....	....	....
....	....	....	....
....	....	....	....
....	....	....	....
....	....	....	....
....	....	....	....
....	....	....	....
....	....	....	....
....	....	....	....

Remember to look through your list again before the exam.

TOPICS AND VOCABULARY 7

This section contains topics which could come up in the examination, especially in Paper 2 (Writing) and Paper 5 (Speaking).

At the top of each right-hand page in this section you will see some questions that you could be asked in the exam. Under these you will see some ideas for answering the questions. You are not expected to use everything you see because some will not be relevant to you. Use the words and expressions as a starting point for **your own ideas.**

To prepare for the exam, take each topic and make your own list of words and expressions. As you come across more items, add them to your list.

Remember the importance of word partnerships. If you are thinking about the topic of **Education and Training,** for example, you could include such expressions as:

take/pass/fail an exam
discipline problems
get the relevant qualification
suitable for beginners
drop out of college
lecture notes

7.1 **Food and Cooking** . . . .

Fill each blank with a suitable word or phrase from the list.
Use each item once only.

add	additives	beat the eggs	list of ingredients
boil	dressing	breakfast cereal	local market
empty	simmer	fast food	low-calorie spread
stir	spices	main course	peel the potatoes
taste	vegetarian	speciality	slice of toast

1. The .... was so filling that I don't think I've got any room for a dessert.

2. I have to watch my figure so I use a .... instead of butter.

3. Over 5 million servings of the nation's favourite .... are eaten every day.

4. At the beginning of every recipe you'll find a ....

5. It certainly looks good but what does it .... like?

6. He's a ...., so this limits the choice of things we can offer him.

7. If you could ...., I'll see to the other vegetables.

8. You must .... thoroughly when you make an omelette.

9. Food bought at the .... is usually much fresher.

10. He loves every kind of ...., especially enormous hamburgers.

11. To make soup from a packet you .... the contents into a saucepan, ... water, ... well, bring the mixture to the .... and allow to .... for five minutes.

12. Fish soup is a .... of this region.

13. The .... on the salad was a little too rich for me.

14. Do you want another .... or can I put the bread away?

15. Some .... are used only to make the food more attractive.

16. In many countries, herbs and .... are often used to add flavour to a dish.

How important is food in your country?
What kind of food do/don't you like?
Describe how to make your favourite dish or a traditional dish from your country.

One of our local/national dishes is called ....

It's (quite/very) spicy/strong ....

It's made from ....

Complete the column on the right with a word from the list below.
Use each word once only. Space has been left for your own examples.

bake   beat   chop   cut   divide
grate   melt   pour   serve   sprinkle

1. .... the meat into thin slices.

2. .... the onion finely.

3. .... some cheese to use as a topping.

4. .... half of the milk into a large bowl.

5. .... the eggs thoroughly.

6. .... the dough into 2 balls.

7. .... the butter in a frying pan.

8. .... in a hot oven.

9. .... sugar over the top of the cake.

10. .... on a warm plate.

....

....

....

....

....

7.2 **Describing People** . . . .

Use a suitable word or phrase from the list below to complete each sentence. Use each item once only.

bald patch	impulsive	shy	have the sense
courage	on a diet	spiteful	look my best
curly hair	parting	upset easily	lose my temper
extrovert	piercing eyes	very proud	speak openly

1. She's always going .... because she has a complex about not being slim enough.

2. Unfortunately she gets .... so be careful what you say.

3. He had medium-length grey hair with a .... down the middle.

4. As I meet a lot of people in my job, I try to ...., which means I spend quite a lot on clothes every year.

5. She's very .... so she keeps doing things she regrets later.

6. As he's tall, you don't notice the .... on top of his head.

7. He was so .... that at parties he never spoke to people unless he had been introduced to them.

8. It takes .... to stand up to somebody who's bullying you.

9. I can .... to her. I don't have to hide my feelings.

10. She had a perm because she thought .... looked fashionable.

11. He's a great .... He loves going out and meeting people.

12. She had .... which seemed to look right through you.

13. She's .... of her son and never stops talking about him.

14. I hope they'll .... to lock the doors and call the police.

15. It was very .... of him to deliberately try to make a fool of her.

16. I'm afraid I seem to .... more often these days, especially when I get bad service.

Look at people in magazine and newspaper pictures, or at people around you.
Describe them.
Describe some of your friends and say why you like them.
Describe somebody you don't like and say why.

Put each of the words or expressions below into an appropriate list.
Add any other words and expressions which you think will be useful when describing people you know or have seen.

attractive   **absent-minded**   **considerate**   **hates making decisions**
clumsy   **short-sighted**   **inquisitive**   **hides her feelings**
dynamic   **wavy brown hair**   **takes risks**   **tends to exaggerate**

POSITIVE	NEGATIVE	EITHER/NEITHER
....	....	....
....	....	....
....	....	....
....	....	....
....	....	....
....	....	....
....	....	....
....	....	....
....	....	....
....	....	....
....	....	....
....	....	....

STUDY TIP   One way of building up the vocabulary you need is to sort words and expressions into such categories as **positive** or **negative**.
Sometimes it is difficult to decide. How would you classify the word **'extrovert'** for example? Look back at other words on the opposite page and decide how you would categorise them.

7.3 **Sport and Hobbies** . . . .

Complete each sentence by using a word or phrase from the list below.
Use each item once only.

championship	explain the rules	lack of support	tactical game
cheer	final score	member	take part in
disqualified	first round	play cards	take up
draw	keen on	sponsor	train really hard

1. He agreed to .... the team provided they put the name of his company on their shirts.

2. You have to .... if you want to get to the top in this sport.

3. They were knocked out in the .... of the competition.

4. She tried to .... to me but I found them very complicated.

5. I've never been very .... jogging, especially at night.

6. In the evening we used to .... but never for money, of course.

7. He was .... after the drug test proved positive.

8. I've decided to .... this year's competition.

9. The spectators began to .... as he ran onto the pitch.

10. It's very expensive to become a .... of the tennis club.

11. Chess is a very .... and you have to think out each move extremely carefully.

12. Both teams played well so a .... was a fair result.

13. The team has a good chance of winning the .... this year.

14. The club had to close due to ....

15. After all that excitement, the .... was one-nil.

16. I decided to .... tennis after my doctor warned me that I was terribly unfit.

What are the most popular sports in your country?
What sports and hobbies are you interested in?
How long have you been doing them?
What do they involve? What equipment do you need?
Where do you do them? Why do you like them?

I think the most popular sports in my country are ....

A lot of people go swimming/riding/sailing/skiing ....

....

Add your own sports and hobbies

I'm interested in	**You need**
photography	spare lenses, a tripod
computing	lots of disks, lots of patience
climbing	good equipment, especially boots
football	a ball and an open space
golf	to join a club, unfortunately
....	....
....	....
....	....
....	....

I first took it up	years ago
	when I was ....
I enjoy it because	**I like being in the fresh air.**
	I can meet lots of interesting people.
	....

7.4 **Law and Order** . . . .

Complete each sentence with a word or phrase from the list below.
Use each item once only.

admit	break in	community service	forged money
arrest	terrorist	on probation	death penalty
fined	vandalised	plead guilty	smuggling drugs
prove	witness	shoplifting	reach a verdict

1. They fitted security locks to make it more difficult for a burglar to ....

2. She was caught trying to buy a video recorder with ....

3. If more offenders did ...., this would benefit local people and reduce overcrowding in prisons.

4. He was put .... as it was his first offence.

5. The phone box had been .... so I looked for another one.

6. One .... was able to give a good description of the thief.

7. In an area of high unemployment, ... can be a problem, especially from supermarkets.

8. He was .... £400 and banned from driving for a year.

9. If you ...., the judge might give you a lighter sentence.

10. They finally got her to .... that she had forged her employer's signature on the form.

11. This is a complex case so the jury may take time to ....

12. In some countries you can be executed for .... like cocaine.

13. There isn't enough evidence to .... that he committed the crime although we're sure it must have been him.

14. The police appeared and started to .... the demonstrators.

15. There's no .... in this country so he'll probably be sentenced to life imprisonment.

16. He may be a .... to you but to other people he's a freedom-fighter.

Look at the list of crimes below.
Which of them do you think are the most serious?
What punishment would you recommend for each one?
Is sending people to prison the best way to beat crime?

Put an explanation next to any difficult words.
Can you add any more crimes to the list?

arson ....

assault ....

blackmail ....

burglary ....

kidnapping ....

selling drugs ....

shoplifting ....

smuggling watches ....

vandalism ....

....

....

....

I think somebody who:

sets fire to a building   **should be sent to prison**

breaks into a house   **should have to do community service**

....

....

....

7.5 **At Home** . . . .

Complete each sentence with a word or phrase from the list below.
Use each item once only.

cellar	landing	share a flat	doing the washing-up
converted	lounge	double glazing	replace the fuse
gadget	terraced	household chores	spare bedroom
installed	wardrobe	lay the table	storage space

1. When my mother came to live with us I had the garage .... into a bed-sitting room.

2. Fitting .... has made the room warmer and reduced noise.

3. Let's have supper in the .... and watch the late-night news.

4. His kitchen is fitted with every kind of .... from a coffee grinder to an electric tin-opener.

5. Since I had a shower .... I've hardly ever had a bath.

6. I only have to .... and the video will be working again.

7. If you could help clear the table, I'll start ....

8. My bedroom has a spacious .... where I hang all my clothes.

9. We live in a .... house so we get noise from the neighbours on both sides.

10. They can easily put her up in their ....

11. Dinner's ready so will you .... ?

12. I really hate dusting, ironing and all the other ....

13. We need some more .... to put all the games and toys away.

14. She left a pile of clothes on the second-floor ....

15. He used to .... with a colleague before he found a place of his own.

16. There's a .... under the house where we store the produce we grow in our garden.

Describe your home.
Describe your room.
Is there anything you'd like to do to improve your house?

I live	in a flat/ semi-detached/detached/terraced house/
	in the centre of town/ in the suburbs
	in a quiet/noisy street
	....

It's got	two bedrooms ....
	....
It hasn't got	a garden ....
	....

My room is	on the ground/first/second floor ....
	at the front/back of the house ....
	opposite ....
	next to ....
	....

In the corner	there's a ....
On the wall	....
Under the window	there are some ....
By the door	....

If I could afford it, I would like to

have	an extension	built to have more space to work in.
	a shower	installed
	....	....

STUDY TIP   Look inside magazines for 'before and after' pictures showing how rooms have been improved. Try to describe what **has been done** to the rooms.

10*

7.6 **Holidays** . . . .

Complete each sentence with a word or phrase from the following list.
Use each item once only.

deposit	change money	activity holiday	entertainment facilities
get a tan	fully insured	holiday resort	sightseeing tour
guest house	put on a show	glossy brochure	tourist information office
make friends	self-catering	package holiday	twin-bedded room

1. Make sure you're .... in case something goes wrong.

2. If you go to such a popular ...., you must expect crowds.

3. Sharing a .... is much cheaper than getting two singles.

4. It's easy to .... when you're on holiday. How many people do you keep in touch with afterwards?

5. We went on a .... so that we didn't have to worry about meals and accommodation. Everything was included.

6. They just lay on the beach all day, trying to ....

7. If you stay at a .... it works out cheaper than at a hotel.

8. Yesterday I went on a .... around the Old Town.

9. Apart from the all-night disco, the .... weren't very good.

10. I was very impressed with the .... they sent me giving details of their sailing holidays.

11. The hotel staff .... every night to entertain the guests.

12. For a family I would recommend ...., especially if they're fussy eaters!

13. The staff in the local .... should be able to tell you what's on in and around town this week.

14. You get a much better rate if you .... at a bank rather than at your hotel.

15. She certainly looks much fitter after her .... !

16. You pay a .... of ten per cent when you book and the balance six weeks before the start of your holiday.

What kind of holiday do you like? Where do you go? What do you do?
Describe your last holiday.
If you could afford it, where would you most like to go on holiday?

For me, the most important thing about a holiday is	making new friends
	doing something completely different
	....
	....

It was	in a busy sea-side resort, with lots of tourists.
	miles from anywhere.
	about five minutes' walk from the town centre.
	....

What I enjoyed most was	going on a trip around the islands.
	exploring the countryside.
	....

The worst	part of the holiday	was	when I lost my passport.
	thing about it		the fact that the beaches were very crowded.
			....

(If I could afford it,)	I'd really love to	tour around North and South America.
		sail round the world for a couple of years.
		hitch-hike round India!
		....

STUDY TIP Look through some travel brochures and compare the holidays and hotels that are advertised. Say which you would prefer and why.

7.7 **Entertainment** . . . .

Complete each sentence with a word or phrase from the list below.
Use each item once only.

---

another channel	**commercials**	**perform live**	**special effects**
cartoon characters	**directed**	**rehearse**	**stars**
choir	**final scene**	**reviews**	**stunt**
clapped	**hit**	**series**	**subtitled**

---

1. Most foreign films are .... although some are dubbed.

2. Most of the money goes on .... when you make a science-fiction film nowadays.

3. The audience .... enthusiastically when the star of the show finally appeared.

4. I've watched the first two programmes but this .... isn't as good as the previous one.

5. In the .... of the film he returns home to his wife.

6. I think the .... on TV are sometimes better than the programmes!

7. They usually .... for at least two months before they take a play on tour.

8. Mickey Mouse is one of the most famous .... in the world.

9. If you don't like the programme, switch to ....

10. Every .... in the film was carefully prepared to make sure that nobody got hurt.

11. Some pop stars don't really want to .... because they don't sound as good as they do on their records.

12. 'North by Northwest' was .... by Alfred Hitchcock.

13. The film .... Cary Grant. He plays a man who is chased by enemy agents who want to kill him because he knows too much.

14. There were so many singers in the .... that I thought for a moment that they wouldn't all get on the stage.

15. She always reads the .... in the newspapers to find out which films and plays are worth seeing.

16. Her first record was such a .... that it will be difficult to repeat its success.

How often do you go to the cinema or theatre?
What kinds of films, plays or shows do you like?
What kinds of TV and radio programmes do you like?
How important is music in your life?
What kind of music do you like?

I like westerns/science fiction/adventure films/musicals.

One of my favourite films is called ....

I can really recommend it.

It stars ....

It's set in ....

It's about .... who ....

....

I like watching/listening to comedy shows/documentaries/serials.

Recently I saw/listened to a programme about ....

....

I suppose music is (quite) important in my life.

Music is(n't) very important to me.

I'm especially fond of classical music/pop music/jazz.

....

7.8 **Education and Training** . . . .

Complete each sentence with a word or phrase from the list below.
Use each item once only.

brush up	diploma	boarding school	course work
cheat	relevant to	co-educational	maintain discipline
enrol for	revise for	sandwich course	secondary school
fees	specialise in	school uniform	under great pressure

1. I went to the local college to .... a course in economics.

2. Some parents who can afford the .... send their children to private schools.

3. In my last years at school we had to .... three subjects and I chose physics, chemistry and mathematics.

4. At the moment I'm studying for my secretarial ....

5. In my country .... is only worn at private schools.

6. He watched us closely during exams so that we didn't ....

7. You have to be really strict to .... with some of the pupils you get nowadays.

8. I went to .... so I only saw my parents during the holidays.

9. I wish I had gone to a .... rather than a single-sex school as I'm sure I wouldn't be so shy when I meet people.

10. We grade pupils on the basis of .... and end-of-term tests.

11. In some countries children are put .... by their parents to get good exam results.

12. The first year I worked at the factory I attended a .... at the local college.

13. The change from primary to .... was quite traumatic for him.

14. Can I borrow your lecture notes? I've got to .... tomorrow's test.

15. I went on a four-week course to .... my English.

16. Is what we're learning really .... the life we're going to lead when we leave school?

What did/do you like about school? Why?
What did/do you dislike about school. Why?
If you were a teacher, what would you do to make your lessons interesting?
What would you do with pupils or students who kept disrupting your lessons?

First, make a list of your school/college subjects:

....

....

....

....

My favourite subject was/is ....

What I really like(d) was/is ....

because ....

....

I'm no good at ....

I've never been any good at ....

What I found/find really boring was/is ....

because ....

If I were a teacher, I'd try to make lessons interesting by ....

....

If a student disrupted the class, I'd ....

....

7.9 **The Environment** . . . .

Complete the passage by using the words and phrases in the list below. Use each item once only.

alternative sources	nuclear waste	research
cut down on	pesticides	rush hour
dramatic increase	polluting	subsidised fares
exhaust fumes	public transport	switch to
food chain	quality of life	traffic jams

Our environment is being destroyed but we still have time to do something about it.

Every day during the **1.** .... you can see cars stuck in

2. .... sending their **3.** ....

up into the atmosphere, **4.** .... our environment. If we had

an integrated **5.** .... system with

6. ...., commuters would be encouraged to leave their cars

at home and **7.** .... a more efficient form of transport.

It is not only in towns that the **8.** .... is being threatened.

Although farmers say they have to spray **9.** .... on their

crops, some experts believe that these chemicals could get into the

10. ...., which will result in a

11. .... in the number of people affected by cancer and

various allergies. More **12.** .... needs to be carried out so

that we can **13.** .... the use of harmful chemicals but still

produce the food we need.

Potentially the most dangerous threat to the environment is **14.** ....

from power stations. Can it really be stored safely? By developing

15. .... of energy, such as wind and wave power, we can

make our world much safer to live in.

Have there been any natural disasters in your country (earthquakes, flooding, severe thunder storms etc)? If so, what happened? What damage was caused?
Can you think of any ways in which pollution is affecting the environment?
What can be done about it?
Are you optimistic or pessimistic about the future? Why?

(Some years ago) there was ....

A lot of buildings	collapsed.
	were destroyed.
	....
Several people	were injured.
	lost their homes.
	....

In the past .... **used to** ....

but now ....

In my opinion,	more research should be carried out.
I believe	dangerous pesticides should be banned.
	....
In addition to this,	**I think**	....
At the same time,		....

I suppose I'm quite optimistic about	the future.
I'm afraid I'm rather pessimistic about	what can be done.
	....

because ....

7.10 **Town and Country** . . . .

Complete each sentence with a word or phrase from the list below.
Use each item once only.

litter	building site	housing estate	blocks of flats
hedge	quiet suburb	main crops	multi-storey car park
outskirts	spoil the view	make way for	pedestrian precinct
rural life	tiny cottage	wander	property prices

1. I've heard that the developers are building 3 more ....

2. Residents of the new .... were complaining about the poor bus service in the evening.

3. They want to turn the town centre into a .... so they're trying to ban all cars from there.

4. This part of town seems to be a vast ...., with office blocks going up everywhere.

5. The new .... can hold up to 1,000 vehicles.

6. When they had nothing to do, they would .... around the shopping centre.

7. Our house is in a .... about 2 miles from the city centre.

8. The hall has been demolished to .... the new sports centre.

9. As they live on the .... of town, they can quite easily go for a walk in the country.

10. The pace of .... seems much slower to people from the city.

11. We don't want tourists leaving .... everywhere as this area has been designated as one of outstanding natural beauty.

12. Wheat is one of the .... grown in this region.

13. The .... that used to separate the two fields has been replaced by a barbed-wire fence.

14. Those electricity pylons completely .... over the valley.

15. She dreamed of retiring to a .... with a beautiful garden.

16. Now that people from the city are buying second homes, ... are too high for most young people from our village.

Describe the place where you live, or a city you know.
What do people do there (work, spare time) ?
Compare life in a town or city with life in the country.

....is │ in the north / south / east / west / middle of my country.

│ by the sea / on a river / in the mountains ....

....

It has a few / several / a lot of ....

....

It's famous for its ....

....

The people who live there work in offices / restaurants. ....

In the evening they usually / sometimes ....

....

City life is (much) │ less relaxing
more strenuous │ than life in the country.

.... │ ....

.... │ ....

In the country: │ while in a big city:

people have time to talk to you │ people are always in a hurry

.... │ ....

.... │ ....

.... │ ....

.... │ ....

7.11 **Travel and Transport** . . . .

Complete each sentence with a word or phrase from the list below.
Use each item once only.

bumpy flight	cut-price fares	luggage rack	serviced
change trains	economy class	more economical	skidded
collided with	get a lift	on board	speed limit
commute	itinerary	reclining seats	unavoidably delayed

1. Those cars must be breaking the .... ! Look at how fast they're going!

2. As the cruise progressed, life .... soon settled down to a comfortable routine.

3. Put your suitcase up on the .... out of the way.

4. We've worked out our .... very carefully to avoid most of the usual hold-ups.

5. The travel agency are offering .... to destinations all over the USA.

6. There was a line of hitch-hikers all hoping to ....

7. You'd better have your car .... before you go on holiday.

8. Although the coach had .... and air-conditioning, I still had difficulty getting to sleep.

9. She chose the smaller car because it was .... on petrol.

10. It was such a .... that at one point the cabin crew had to stop serving dinner and fasten their seatbelts.

11. As I .... to work every day, I've bought a season ticket.

12. The coach .... on some oil and overturned.

13. The flight has been .... due to bad weather.

14. We had to .... at a tiny station in the middle of nowhere.

15. When you fly ...., you don't get so much leg room.

16. One car had .... another and they needed heavy lifting equipment to pull them apart.

What are the advantages and disadvantages of travelling by car, coach, plane, shop and train?
Have you ever had a bad experience when travelling somewhere? If so, what happened?

The main (dis)advantage of travelling by .... **is that**

you	**can**
	can't ....
	(don't) have to

| **On the other hand,** | **if you travel by** .... |
| **However,** | .... |

The worst thing that has ever happened to me while travelling was when I

....

Some friends are coming to stay with you but don't know how to get to your home. They are travelling by car. Write a letter giving them directions.

Go along/up/down ....

as far as/until you get to ....

Turn left/right at/just before/after ....

You'll see .... **on the corner.**

Take the first/second/third etc on the left/right.

My house is on the left/right. It's the one with ....

My flat is on the first/second/top floor ....

If you get lost, you've got my phone number so you can give me a ring.

I'm really looking forward to seeing you again.

See you on ....

7.12 **Work** . . . .

Complete each sentence with a word or phrase from the list below.
Use each item once only.

ambitious	fire	manual work	resign
assembly line	fringe benefit	night shift	responsibility
commission	good impression	permanent post	retire
deal with	job satisfaction	promoted	work overtime

1. It's my .... to see that the goods are delivered on time.

2. Her work was so good that she was .... to the position of assistant manager only a year after she joined the company.

3. Employees have to .... at 65 although I'm sure some would like to stay on.

4. He's finally found a .... working for a pharmaceutical company after years of going from job to job.

5. I've decided to .... and look for a job where I can make more use of my training.

6. As a salesperson, I get .... on every dress I sell.

7. The staff agreed to .... so that the order would be completed on time.

8. The boss threatened to .... her if her work didn't improve.

9. Work on the .... was so monotonous that some employees tried to sabotage it just to have a bit of variety.

10. As I work on the .... I don't have much social life.

11. She's very .... and will do anything to get to the top.

12. You can create a .... before your interview by filling in your application form as neatly as possible.

13. The only ...., or 'perk', he gets is a free company car.

14. In my job I have to .... inquiries from customers.

15. For me .... is more important than a high salary so I'm thinking of becoming a social worker.

16. Who wants an office job when I can earn more by doing ...., like working on a building site?

If you have a job, describe it and say what you like/dislike about it.
If you could do any kind of job, what would you most like to be?
You have seen an advertisement for an English-speaking guide to take groups of tourists around your country. Write a letter of application for the job.

I think I would like to be a(n) ....

because ....

I would like to apply for the job of tourist guide, as advertised in ....

At present I am studying .... at ....

and I hope to ....

For the last .... years I have been working as a(n) ....

for ....

My duties include (+ ing) ....

I have had experience in (+ ing) ....

In previous jobs I have had to ....

I can speak/write/understand English ....

I am applying for the job because ....

....

I would be available for an interview ....

I hope you will consider my application favourably.

I look forward to hearing from you.

7.13 **Describing a Festival** . . . .

Complete each blank with one of the following words or phrases.
Use each item once only.

attracts	erected	commemorate	colourful procession
held	sponsored	local event	street entertainers
floats	stalls	puppet shows	tourist attraction
lasts	dress up	opening ceremony	traditional crafts

Every year a festival is **1.** .... to **2.** .... the founding of our town over 150 years ago. The festival **3.** .... for a week and during that time many local people **4.** .... in old-fashioned clothes, sometimes even wearing them at work.

On the first day of the celebrations an **5.** .... is performed by a visiting celebrity at the band-stand in the town centre. From there a **6.** .... makes its way through the streets of the town. We spend weeks beforehand preparing the **7.** ...., many of which are **8.** .... by local firms and organisations. In addition to these floats, there are bands and **9.** ...., such as fire-eaters, jugglers and clowns walking on stilts.

The procession ends up in the park, where a large marquee has been **10.** .... Around the marquee there are various **11.** .... where you can buy local produce or play traditional games.

Throughout the week many events are organised to recreate life 150 years ago. You can have your photograph taken wearing 19th century clothes or learn **12.** .... such as basket-weaving. For the children there are **13.** .... and talent contests.

The festival **14.** .... thousands of visitors, and what used to be just a small **15.** .... has now grown into a major **16.** ....

Describe an annual festival held either in your town or another part of your country or describe a national festival or holiday.

The festival	is held	....
	takes place	....
	is organised	....
		....

| It | commemorates | .... |
| | celebrates | .... |

We are not sure when/why the festival started but ....

....

Preparations begin many weeks beforehand.

Floats	have to be	decorated.
Decorations		put up.
		....

The streets are	decorated with	....
	lined with	....
	crowded with	....
	....	....

People come from	the surrounding district	to see all the events.
	all over the world	....
	....	....

They	wear	....
	dress up in	....
	take part in	....
	make their way to	....
		....

11*

7.14 **Shopping and Services** . . . .

Use these words to complete the sentences. Use each item once only.

bargain	faulty goods	out of stock	insurance company
go with	local shops	can't afford	get a discount
loan	on credit	street market	rate of exchange
refund	try it on	take it back	window shopping

1. This coat was a .... ! I got it for half the usual price.

2. Unfortunately, we are unable to supply the item you ordered as it is temporarily ....

3. The butcher's, the baker's, the greengrocer's and other .... lost customers after the new supermarket opened.

4. I'm not sure if this dress is the right size. Can I .... ?

5. We .... a new car so we're looking for a second-hand one in good condition.

6. This CD player I bought doesn't work properly. – Well, ... then!

7. We got a favourable .... at the bank because our currency is quite strong at the moment.

8. I'm looking for some trousers to .... this jacket.

9. I asked my bank manager for a .... but he turned me down.

10. We can only replace .... if you have a receipt.

11. Every Saturday there was a .... in the centre of town.

12. They spent the morning .... as they couldn't afford to buy anything.

13. The .... refused to pay the claim as they believed the shopkeeper had started the fire deliberately.

14. You'll .... of ten per cent if you show your student card.

15. They couldn't replace the camera so they gave me a ....

16. Mail-order shopping grew in popularity because it was convenient and you could buy items ....

A new shopping centre, including a hypermarket, is going to be built on the outskirts of town. What effects will it have?
What kind of clothes do you like wearing? Where do you usually buy them?
You have had a problem with a faulty product or bad service. Make a complaint.
Think about when, where, what happened, what you want done.

The new shopping centre may take trade away from neighbourhood and town centre shops e.g. the grocer's / ....

It will be better for car owners because ....

....

I like wearing casual / smart / fashionable clothes. / I'm not very interested in fashion ....

....

What I like wearing most is / are ....

It's / They're made of .... and has / have ....

....

I buy most of my clothes in big department stores / small boutiques / in street markets / from

mail-order catalogues ....

I bought (item) .... (date) ....

Unfortunately ....

....

I went to your restaurant / hotel ....

The food was / the room was / the staff were ....

....

Could you please replace it / repair it / refund my money / look into this matter for me ....

7.15 **Health and Fitness** . . . .

Complete each sentence with a word or phrase from the list below. Use each item once only.

come out in	keep fit	private patient	stress-related
health service	operate on	recover from	successfully treated
highly infectious	outbreak	regular exercise	upset stomach
injured	spread	relieve the pain	visiting hours

1. We go jogging every morning to ....

2. He took some time to .... the effects of the anaesthetic.

3. Hospital .... are from 2 to 4 in the afternoon and from 6 to 8 in the evening.

4. Six people were killed and twenty .... in the accident.

5. I think my .... was due to nerves, not something I'd eaten.

6. As a ...., I can choose when to have my operation.

7. This medicine should .... and help you to get to sleep.

8. Unless more money is provided for the ...., hospital waiting lists will continue to grow.

9. There could be an .... of cholera if they drink any contaminated water.

10. The spots .... from his chest to the rest of his body.

11. The disease is .... so she's in an isolation ward.

12. Many patients have been .... with this drug since it was introduced two years ago.

13. They'll have to .... my arm again if it doesn't improve.

14. I'm allergic to strawberries. They make me .... a rash.

15. I'm getting more and more patients with .... symptoms. Life is really much too hectic these days.

16. If you take .... and cut down on the number of cakes and sweets you eat, you'll feel much healthier.

Do people in your country worry about their health and keeping fit?
Do you do anything to stay healthy? If so, what?
What advice would you give to someone who suffers from stress?
Think of other medical problems and give advice.

To keep fit and healthy I am careful about what I eat / go to aerobics classes / do a lot of sport / go jogging every day / play squash ....

....

Match the problem on the left with the advice on the right. Use each item once only. Write your answers in the boxes. Add more problems and advice of your own in the space provided.

A: What's the matter?
What's wrong?
What's up?
You don't look very well.

B: I've got ....   **A:** If I were you, I'd ....
You'd better ....
Maybe you should ....

1. backache	a. get a walking stick.
2. a cut finger	b. buy one of those nasal sprays.
3. dandruff	c. put some cream on it and cover up.
4. indigestion	d. clean it thoroughly with antiseptic.
5. a blocked nose	e. bend your knees when you lift things.
6. a sore throat	f. try one of those special shampoos.
7. a swollen ankle	g. gargle and try not to talk so much.
8. sunburn	h. eat more slowly.

1	
2	
3	
4	
5	
6	
7	
8	

I suffer from stress ....

I've got a ....

....

....

7.16 **Science and Technology** . . . .

Use these words to complete the sentences. Use each item once only.

database	genetic engineering	computer networks	come to terms with
made redundant	repetitive tasks	life expectancy	labour-saving devices
mass-produced	safety features	locate resources	major breakthrough
monitor	strict safeguards	under development	taken for granted

1. As more and more of us are linked by .... , how soon will it be before the paperless office becomes a reality?

2. This new technique is a .... in the treatment of cancer.

3. The dish-washer and other .... have helped to relieve the boredom of domestic chores.

4. Satellite technology can help to .... for extraction from the earth.

5. The Model T Ford was the first .... car in the world.

6. It is difficult for some people to .... the speed of change in the modern world.

7. The police have access to a vast .... which helps them in their fight against crime.

8. We need .... to prevent all the information stored on computers from being misused.

9. Many .... which people found boring and tiring can now be carried out by machines.

10. Many employees have been .... as a result of the introduction of new technology.

11. Nuclear power stations have computer-controlled systems to .... their reactors and prevent accidents.

12. This car comes with such .... as a collapsible steering column and a driver's airbag.

13. A power station capable of producing electricity from waves is currently ....

14. With the advances in .... we may be able to create a race of "perfect" human beings one day, or is that just science fiction?

15. The increase in .... has led to problems such as how to pay for the care of the elderly.

16. Many technological developments which have greatly affected the way we live are nowadays .... by the younger generation.

How have science and technology changed our lives? Think about discoveries, inventions, new products, and their effects (good and bad).
How will science and technology affect our lives in the future?

Scientific and technological breakthroughs have brought great benefits. You only have to look around your own home to see ....
....

Many illnesses can now be treated or cured, for example, ...
....

Other examples of changes are ....
....

Have our lives always been improved, however? Have we become too passive? Are we too dependent on technology? How dangerous could it be?

Take, for example, television / computer games / the Internet ....
....
....

New products have also made a major difference to our working lives.

Nowadays, ...
....

In the future there may be even more major breakthroughs in the fields of medicine / leisure / work ....
....

We may no longer have to ....
....

We will be able to ....
....

7.17 **The Family and Relationships** . . . .

Use these words to complete the sentences. Use each item once only.

acquaintance	divorce rate	house on fire	break the ice
backgrounds	foster homes	civil ceremony	for the sake of
date	make friends	good company	gets on my nerves
in common	split up	on speaking terms	happily married

1. In the UK you can have either a religious or .... when you get married.

2. The way Hannah slams the door really ....

3. We played some games to .... and get the party going.

4. Joe isn't exactly a friend of mine. He's more of an ....

5. There can be problems sustaining a relationship if people come from different social and cultural ....

6. With the increase in the .... , the number of one-parent families has shot up.

7. Are Dave and Ann still going out?
   Haven't you heard? They .... a couple of months ago.

8. We never argue. In fact, we get on like a .... all the time.

9. It was so easy to .... as everyone was so helpful and hospitable.

10. I'm afraid I'm not very .... tonight. I've got a lot on my mind.

11. Lucie and I get on really well. We've got so much ....

12. Damien's mother wasn't capable of looking after him so he lived in a series of .... for the next few years.

13. Andy and Sue are only staying together .... the children.

14. Max hasn't been .... with his neighbours since their tree fell into his garden and caused all that damage.

15. Why is Bill spending so long in the bathroom?
    He's got a .... with his new girlfriend this evening.

16. On the surface they seemed to be a .... couple but in fact they were always having rows.

How has family life changed since your grandparents were young?
What makes a relationship successful?
Why do relationships fail?

In the past the family unit was much bigger/children used to respect their parents/ ....

....

Nowadays one-parent families are more common/there seem to be more problems with

discipline / ....

Decide whether the following comments are positive or negative

1. They're always at each other's throats.
2. They're devoted to each other.
3. I can't stand him.
4. We're firm friends.
5. We've never really hit it off.
6. That's a very condescending attitude.
7. I've got a soft spot for him.
8. He's fallen for her.
9. She broke the engagement off.
10. I think we've grown apart.
11. He walked out on her.
12. He's constantly nagging me.
13. I'll always stand by you.
14. I'm quite fond of her.
15. We've fallen out.
16. They're like chalk and cheese!

Make some true statements about yourself using some of the above expressions:

....

....

....

....

Can you list any other ways of describing successful and unsuccessful relationships?

Successful Relationships

....

....

....

....

Unsuccessful Relationships

....

....

....

....

7.18 **The Media** . . . .

Complete each sentence with a word or phrase from the list below. Use each item once only.

editorial	news flash	cable television	current affairs
headline	pick up	live coverage	increase circulation
in depth	speculation	press conference	respect for privacy
obituary	spokesperson	special issue	unbiased account

1. In an attempt to .... the editor decided to print more "human interest" stories.

2. The company held a .... to launch their new range.

3. This channel is devoted solely to news and ....

4. With this short-wave radio I can .... broadcasts from all over the world.

5. There has been a lot of .... in the press that the minister is about to resign.

6. This month there's a .... of the magazine with information and advice about going on holiday.

7. We live in a mountainous region so if it wasn't for .... we wouldn't receive any broadcasts of a reasonable quality.

8. We interrupt this programme to bring you an important ....

9. Exclusively on this channel we have .... of the big match.

10. Next morning an .... appeared in the newspaper, criticising the government's defence policy.

11. These reports are so subjective. Where can I find an .... of what happened?

12. The President's .... was not at all flattering and his widow was extremely upset.

13. There, right on the front page, was the .... , ANOTHER RISE IN UNEMPLOYMENT.

14. Some tabloid journalists have no .... I'm sure my telephone has been bugged!

15. A .... interviewed on the local news denied that the company was in any way responsible for the accident.

16. In our evening bulletin we try to report on the news .... by providing more background information.

How many television channels can you receive in your country? What kinds of programmes do they broadcast?
What different types of newspapers and magazines are there in your country? Compare the news you get from television with the news you read in newspapers. What are the advantages and disadvantages of the two media?

Most people can receive .... channels. If you have cable television / a satellite dish, ...

....

One channel broadcasts mainly / is devoted to sports programmes / news and current affairs / light entertainment programmes /..

for example, ...

We have .... so-called quality newspapers: ....

The most right-wing paper is .... and the most left-wing paper is ....

The best of the tabloid / popular papers is .... because ....

The worst paper is .... because .... I read ....

because ....

There are a lot of magazines published every month. My favourite ones are ....

because .... I subscribe to .... It's ....

On television, the pictures are very important / some programmes have to be sensational to keep the advertisers happy. ....

....

Newspapers, on the other hand, can report events in more depth / are less visual ....

....

STUDY TIP   Reading articles and news reports in English will help you to prepare for the exam, especially for Paper 1 (Reading). Try to buy or borrow newspapers and magazines in English regularly and get into the habit of reading them as quickly as possible.
Can you receive radio or TV broadcasts in English? If so, use them to improve your listening comprehension.

7.19 **The Weather** . . . .

Complete each sentence with a word or phrase from the list below. Use each item once only.

changeable	dark clouds	bitterly cold	global warming
cut off	heavy rain	gust of wind	struck by lightning
hot spell	turned out	mild climate	weather forecast
sticky	we're in for	pouring down	widespread damage

1. This area has got a fairly .... so we didn't expect the temperature to fall so sharply.

2. A .... blew my hat off and sent it flying across the road.

3. Tomorrow's weather will be .... with sunny periods and scattered showers.

4. The rain came .... and we got soaked to the skin.

5. Some scientists claim that the unusual weather is the result of ....

6. The hurricane swept through the islands, causing ....

7. Many villages were .... by heavy snow drifts and emergency supplies had to be taken in by helicopter.

8. That blackened tree over there was .... during a violent thunderstorm.

9. It was so hot and .... during the day that we soon got worn out if we tried to do any hard physical work.

10. If this .... continues, water will have to be rationed.

11. In the distance, ... covered the sky and you could hear the rumble of thunder.

12. It's .... nice again, hasn't it?
    – Yes, it has. Let's hope it lasts.

13. It looks as if .... a spell of showery weather over the next few days.

14. It was so .... that I kept the central heating at maximum and put on a heavy pullover.

15. Due to .... the pitch was flooded and the match had to be abandoned.

16. According to the ...., the maximum temperature today should be about thirty degrees.

Describe the climate of your country. Does it vary from region to region?
What is the weather like today? What is the forecast for tomorrow and the
outlook for the next few days?
Have you ever had a good or bad experience as a result of the weather? If so,
describe what happened.

The climate in my country varies a lot according to the season / doesn't change very much

except ....

(In the spring / summer / autumn / winter) it is (often / usually / sometimes) very hot / bitterly cold

....

The temperature can reach as high as / fall as low as ....

We have a lot of thunderstorms / snow ....

....

Tomorrow it will / should be sunny / cloudy / changeable ....

There will be scattered showers / dense fog ....

The maximum / minimum temperature will be ....

It didn't rain for months. As a result, ...

....

One night there was a terrible storm / hurricane / gale / blizzard ....

....

It was so hot / cold that ....

....

STUDY TIP Remember that a description of the weather could be an important part of
a composition in the examination. Make a list of different types of weather and the effect
they can have on people, the environment and everyday life.

7.20 **Your Own Country** . . . .

Describe your own country. Answer these questions as fully as you can:
What is the population of your country? What sort of place is it - hilly?
mountainous? flat? lots of lakes? Are the different regions very different from
each other? What are the four major cities? Why are they important? What are
the main industries? What about exports? What is your country most famous for?

We have a population of around .... million, bigger than .... ,
but smaller than .... To the north lies ...., to the south is
...............................; .... is to the east and .... is to the west.
The people in the north/west have a reputation for being a bit ...., but in the
south/east the people are much more ....

.... is a (very) hilly / mountainous / flat country. The highest mountain is
................................, and the most important river is the .... Another
important feature of my country is .... The climate is ....
When you talk to people about ...., they tend to think of places like
.... and ...., which are very .... But there
are also places like .... and ...., which are
.... and .... and well worth visiting.

The main regions are .... Of these the most important is
................................, because .... The main cities are the capital
................................, and .... If you could only spend a day / weekend / week
in ...., I would recommend you visit .... and go to
.... You should also make sure you see .... And the
.... is not to be missed! The city I like best is .... because
.... I was born in .... and my mother and
father come from .... The best place to go on holiday in ....
is ...., because ...., but don't go in .... as it
gets very hot / crowded.

Our main exports include ....
.... is / are grown in ....
.... is / are produced in ....

Ask people the name of a famous .... and they'll probably say
................................, but we also have .... who is / was famous for
.... The thing my country is most famous for is .... The
thing I am most proud of in my country is ....

Useful Words and Phrases

big city   university / market / seaside / town   little village
industrial / agricultural area   tourist spot   commercial / cultural centre
peaceful   relaxing   busy   picturesque   modern   traditional   cosmopolitan

WRITING AND SPEAKING

8

In units 8.1 to 8.6 of this section you will practise the language which will be useful when you do the writing exam. In 8.7 you will see examples of the type of questions you could be asked in the examination.

In Paper 2 the examiners will be looking for:

Accuracy in grammar, spelling and punctuation
Good organisation of your ideas
Appropriate vocabulary
Appropriate register

You will have to think about the purpose of what you are writing and the effect it will have on the target audience. This will affect the information you include and the type of language you use.

Read the questions carefully and make sure you answer every part of those you decide to do. In Part 1 (the compulsory task), for example, you should cover all the points in the information you are given.

It is a good idea to spend a few minutes thinking about what you are going to write. Make a few notes in which you organise your ideas and list some of the vocabulary and structures you can use.

One of the main ideas in this book is that you should learn how words go together in partnerships. This idea is very important if you want to write something which is interesting to read. Look at this sentence:

He walked up to the front door.

What a BORING sentence! HOW did he walk? WHAT KIND OF front door was it? Think of some words.

He walked reluctantly up to the enormous front door.

Don't be too clever and fill your writing with lots of colourful vocabulary, but do think about the way in which words go together. If you can show that you know how to use language in this way, you will do much better in the examination.

In units 8.8 to 8.10 you will see advice and expressions to help you prepare for Paper 5 (Speaking).

8.1 **Writing – Capital Letters** . . . .

Mark the places where capital letters are needed in each sentence.

EXERCISE 1   Make all the capitals in this way: ⌐london

---

1. when they fly to switzerland they always take a swissair flight from london.

2. at christmas they stayed at a french hotel and at new year they stayed at a scottish hotel.

3. the grand hotel is famous for its restaurant.

4. princess diana is queen elizabeth's daughter-in-law.

5. my favourite horror film is 'bride of frankenstein'.

6. he was born on a wednesday morning in the middle of february.

7. the capital of the united states is washington.

8. last summer i went to germany to learn german at a language school.

EXERCISE 2   Put full stops and capital letters where necessary in this passage.

---

as it was january and the middle of summer, the sun was beating down as the passengers got

on the plane some time after it had taken off, the pilot made an announcement: "this is

captain davis speaking if there is a doctor on board, could he or she inform a member of the

cabin staff?" when she heard this, maria called a steward, who took her to the back of the

plane there she found a german passenger, who was obviously in great pain it was clear that he

was suffering from appendicitis and needed to get to a hospital the captain decided to divert

the plane to darwin from the airport the passenger was taken by ambulance to the nearest

hospital, where surgeons successfully removed his appendix

Below you will see information about when to use capital letters in English. When there is a space, write another example of your own.

Capital letters are used for:

1. The pronoun "I".

2. The beginning of a sentence:

   Look! It's raining!

3. The beginning of a letter, after the greeting:

   Dear David,

   Thank you for your letter ....

4. The names of:

people:	**Jenny Johnson**
places:	**New York, Madrid**
rivers:	**the Thames, the Nile**
mountains:	**Mount Everest Mont Blanc**

5. Countries, languages and nationalities (fill in your own):

   Finland   **I speak Finnish.**   **I'm a Finn.**   **I eat Finnish food.**

   ....

6. Days, months and festivals but not seasons:

   Tuesday   **February**   **New Year**   but winter

   ....

7. The names of businesses, hotels, restaurants etc:

   a **Lufthansa** flight **Levi** jeans ....

   the **Hotel Splendid** .... (a hotel you know)

   the **Lotus Restaurant** .... (a restaurant you know)

8. Titles of books, plays, films etc.

   (Notice which words do not have capital letters in these examples.)

   Dress-making for Beginners   The Light in the Forest

8.2 **Writing – Linking Words** . . . .

EXERCISE 1 Fill each blank with a word or phrase from the list below. Use each item once only.

although	but	so that	when
as if	if	that	which
because	just as	unfortunately	while
before	so	until	who

Several years ago some friends and I decided to go cycling together. We waited

1. .... the rush hour was over 2. .... we set off.

3. .... it looked 4. .... it was going to rain, we still decided to go

5. .... this was the last opportunity we would have for some time. We had

packed plastic macs 6. .... we wouldn't get too wet 7. .... there

was a shower. 8. .... we were riding along in single file on the outskirts of town,

Paul, 9. .... was bringing up the rear as usual, suddenly gave a shout.

10. .... we turned back to see what was wrong, we found 11. ....

he had swerved to avoid a dog 12. .... had run out in front of him.

13. .... he had gone into a ditch at the side of the road. The bicycle had hardly

been damaged 14. .... Paul was 15. .... bruised and shaken that

we decided to go home. 16. .... we arrived at my house, it started pouring with

rain. We realised that our day out would have ended badly even without the accident.

Look at the way the ideas are linked together in the passage.
Notice also the tenses that are used in this kind of writing.

EXERCISE 2   Choose a word or phrase from the following list to complete the sentences. Use each item once only.

as long as	**by the time**	**in case**	**unless**
as soon as	**even though**	**just as**	**where**

1. They finally arrived home .... the clock was striking twelve.

2. Work stopped .... the bell rang.

3. The workmen had all gone .... I got home.

4. She said she would only go .... he came as well.

5. They used to play football every Saturday .... the weather conditions made it impossible.

6. He didn't wear a coat .... it was freezing outside.

7. A crowd had gathered .... the procession was due to pass.

8. I decided to take my coat .... it got cold later in the day.

EXERCISE 3   Now do the same with these sentences.

Because of this	**Eventually**	**Meanwhile**	**On the other hand**
Despite this	**Luckily**	**Naturally**	**Some time later**

1. The little girl ran out into the street. ...., there weren't any cars coming, or she might have been killed.

2. He suddenly told us he had found a new job. ...., we were all very pleased and congratulated him.

3. She walked slowly towards her house. ...., the burglar was escaping through the back window.

4. We spent the afternoon looking for somewhere to stay. ...., just as we were giving up hope, we saw a sign outside a big old house.

5. Sue worked hard and usually felt very tired when she came home. ...., she hardly ever went out in the evening.

6. It was one of the coldest days of the year. ...., a huge crowd had gathered outside the town hall.

7. You could try writing to him. ...., you might as well wait until you see him again next week.

8. They said goodbye and he never saw her again. ...., he heard that she had married a much older man.

8.3 **Writing – An Informal Letter** . . . .

Fill each blank with the following words. Use each item once only.

As you know	**Anyway**	**in the end**	**get on**
Best wishes	**Congratulations**	**really busy**	**let me know**
I'm sorry	**Thanks**	**of course**	**put you up**

Dear Pete,

1. .... for your last letter. **2.** .... it's taken me so long to reply but I've been **3.** .... moving into my new flat.

4. .... on passing your driving test first time. Now all you have to do is save up for that Porsche you've always wanted – and the tax and insurance, **5.** .... !

6. ...., I've just started a new job as the manager of the biggest video shop in town. I was a bit nervous on my first day when I had to meet the staff, but,

7. ...., everything turned out all right and I think we're going to

8. .... very well.

9. ...., the main reason I'm writing is to invite you to a party I'm having Saturday week. I do hope you can come. I've got a spare bed so I could **10.** .... for the night.

I must stop now or I'll miss the last post. Please **11.** .... if you can come so that I can give you all the details of how to get here.

12. ....

Here are some examples of the types of informal letter you might have to write with useful language for each one. Can you think of more kinds of informal letter?

Starting the letter
Thanks for your letter.
It was wonderful to hear from you again.
I'm sorry I haven't written before, but I've been very busy (-ing).

A Thank-you letter
I just had to write to thank you for (the wonderful party on Saturday).
Thanks very much for (putting me up last weekend).
It was very kind of you to (offer me the use of your flat in Paris.)

Giving advice
In your letter you said you weren't sure what to do about (Jenny). Well, if I were you, I'd (talk things over with her face to face.)
Have you thought about (changing your job?)

Giving good news
I'm sure you'll be pleased to hear that (Jane's expecting a baby in June.)
By the way, did you know that (I'm now manager?)
You'll never guess what happened the other day! (Peter asked me to marry him.)

Giving bad news
I'm sorry to tell you that (I've just lost my job.)
Bad news, I'm afraid. (I've got to go into hospital next week.)

Asking for help
I hope it's not too much to ask, but (could I come and see you next week?)
I wonder if I could ask a favour. Could you (lend me £50 till I'm paid at the end of the month?)

Apologising
I'm writing to say sorry for (what I said last night.) I wasn't thinking. It was very silly of me.
I want to apologise for (ruining your new sofa. I know you said it didn't matter, but it was very clumsy of me to spill my drink all over it.)

Finishing a letter
Well, that's all for now.
I'll tell you more when I see you next week.
Thanks again (for last weekend.)
I'm really looking forward to seeing you again.
See you on (the fifteenth.)

Giving regards
Give my regards to (Mary). Best wishes ...
Look after yourself. Best regards ...
Take care. Yours ...

8.4 **Writing – A More Formal Letter** . . . .

Use the words below to complete the letter. Use each item once only.

grateful	current issue	additional charge	particularly interested
However	eligible for	look forward to	under what circumstances
mentioned	package holidays	send me information	With reference to

Dear Sir or Madam

1. .... your advertisement in the **2.** .... of "Summer

Holiday" magazine, could you please **3.** .... about the holidays you offer

in the United States? I am **4.** .... in your **5.** .... to

California and Florida.

In your advertisement you state that there are reduced prices for children but it is not clear

6. .... these reductions can be obtained. We are a family of four, with two

adults and two children, aged 10 and 16. Could you tell me whether my 16-year-old child

would still be **7.** .... a reduction or if he is now classed as an adult?

Your advertisement also **8.** .... that a free hire car was included in the

holidays in the United States. **9.** ...., there was no information about

insurance. I would be **10.** ...., therefore, if you could inform me whether

this is included or not. If it is not, I would like to know how much the

11. .... would be.

I hope you will be able to answer my queries. I **12.** .... hearing from you.

Yours faithfully

Here are some examples of the types of more formal letter you might have to write. Can you think of any more?

The beginning and the ending
Dear Sir/Madam
Yours faithfully

Dear Mr/Ms/Miss Jones
Yours sincerely

Answering an advertisement
With reference to your advert in the current issue of (Gardening Weekly.)
I have read your advertisement in the July issue of (Classic Cars.)
In your advertisement you state that the Everest Mountain Bike is available in black, white and silver. Could you confirm that silver is currently in stock?

Referring to a letter
Thank you for your letter of (December 3rd) giving me information about (the Safelight.)

Confirming details
I am writing to confirm my telephone order of this morning. I would like to order (one copy of Butterflies of Brazil) and I enclose my credit card details.
I would like to confirm my booking of (one double room) for (three) nights, arriving on (Thursday 15th July), and leaving on (Sunday 18th).

Asking for something
I would be grateful if you would (send me a copy of your current seed catalogue.)
Could you possibly (send me details of your pony-trekking holidays in the Lake District.)

Thanking
Thank you once again for all your help.
I would like to thank you for (the help you gave us when our car broke down.)
Thank you for (making our holiday in York such an enjoyable experience.)

Complaining
I am writing to complain about (the very poor service I received in the Leeds branch of your organisation.)
(Last week I brought an RT170 from your shop in Reading.) It is not working and I would like to return it for a full refund. As I live some distance away, I would be obliged if you would arrange to collect it from the above address.

Endings
I hope you will give this matter your immediate attention.
I look forward to hearing from you as soon as possible.

STUDY TIP If possible, look at advertisements in British or American magazines and newspapers. Use the information to write letters of enquiry. Think about what could go wrong and write letters of complaint.

8.5 **Writing – Organising Your Ideas** . . . .

Before doing a writing task in the exam you should spend a few minutes making sure you understand what you have to do and planning what you are going to write.

Sometimes the question itself will help you with your plan by telling you what points you have to cover. In other cases, for example when you write a narrative, you will have to work out your own plan.

Here are some examples to get you thinking about the possible elements of different writing tasks. Can you think of any more ideas?

NARRATIVE

Make sure that you answer the question written on the exam paper. Don't invent your own question. Among the things to consider are:

1. **Where and when did the events take place?**
2. **Who was involved?** (Physical description? Character?)
3. **What was happening before the event?**
4. **What happened?**
5. **What were the effects of what happened?** (e.g people's reactions, how you felt/feel about it now)

REPORTS AND ARTICLES

1. **Introduction**   What are you writing about?

2. **Give examples of:**
   – what happens and why
   – what people think etc.

> MAKE SURE YOU COVER ALL THE POINTS IN THE QUESTION ! !

3. **Conclusion**   What is your overall impression (favourable or not)?
   What are your recommendations?

OPINION

1. **Introduction**   What is the problem?
   Why is it a problem? (Background information)

2. **The Argument**   List and justify the arguments for one side/solution
   List and justify the counter-arguments
   OR   List possible solutions and their advantages and disadvantages

3. **Conclusion**   Opinion (based on what has gone before)
   OR   Why it is difficult to give an opinion

8.6 Useful Expressions for Reports and Articles

Here are some expressions for the tasks involving reports, articles, and giving opinions.

Purpose
The purpose of this report is to (set out the main arguments in favour of the new bridge.)
In this report I aim to (justify the decision to build the Tunnel.)
My main aim in writing this report is to (clarify the issues surrounding the new by-pass.)

Stating the problem
There has been a lot of controversy recently about the issue of (global warming.)
One of the biggest problems facing the world today is (what to do with nuclear waste.)
During the last few years people have become increasingly worried about (the problem of teenage drug abuse.)

Examples and possibilities
Firstly …
In the first place, …
The most obvious example of (waste) is (the lack of paper recycling plants.)
One possible solution is to (involve the local community more.)
In addition to (last week's television adverts) we are organising (a massive press campaign.)
Another example of (the sheer amount of waste) is the way in which (public bodies simply refuse to do anything about paper recycling.)

Results and effects
(Parental misuse of alcohol) can often result in (children experimenting with drugs.)
One effect of (lowering the age) would be that (more young people would have access to alcohol.)
If we (lowered the age) this would mean that (more young people would experiment with drugs.)

Arguments
Some people would argue that (this is a good thing.) Nevertheless, the fact of the matter is that (the vast majority would be against it.) Although it is true that (more cars mean more pollution), we have to keep in mind that (raising the tax on cars will mean fewer jobs in the car industry.)

Concluding
In conclusion …   To sum up …
It would appear that there is agreement on this issue.
It is clear, therefore, that (only one course of action is possible.)
For this reason I believe that …
It is difficult to decide what the best solution to the problem would be.

8.7 Writing – Possible Topics . . . .

In the writing exam, there are different kinds of writing, such as an informal letter, a report, or an article giving your opinion. You may be given information such as an advertisement to base your answer on. Remember to read the question carefully and write on that topic. Here are some possible topics. Try writing between 120 and 180 words for each task. You should try to do each task in 45 minutes.

1. An informal letter to a friend
a. Invite him / her to a party. Give directions.
b. Tell him / her about your new job.
c. Invite him / her to come on holiday with you.
d. Reply to a wedding invitation. You can't come but would like to call round with a present.
e. Give advice to a friend who is worried about taking the First Certificate exam in a month's time.
f. Describe how to make a traditional dish from your country.

2. A more formal letter
a. Write to a hotel enquiring about accommodation for three adults and two children. One of the adults uses a wheelchair.
b. Write to the manager of a restaurant complaining about the bad service you and your friends received yesterday.
c. Write to the head of the local police asking if someone will come to your school to give a talk about crime prevention.
d. Write to your local newspaper objecting to plans to build houses on part of a local park.
e. Write to members of your local Photographic Society - of which you are the Secretary - giving information about an excursion to the National Film Museum.

3. A Report
a. Write a report on sporting, leisure, and entertainment facilities in your town or area. If necessary make recommendations to improve the situation.
b. Write a report on the food that young people eat. Is it healthy enough? If not, how can they be persuaded to improve their diet?
c. Write a report on a holiday resort you have been to. Would you recommend it?

4. A Story
a. Write a story ending with the words: "I've never been so glad to see anyone in my whole life!"
b. Write a story starting with the words: "As we boarded the plane at 9 o'clock in the morning, we had no idea what lay ahead of us."
c. Write about a day in your life when everything went wrong.

5. Your Opinion
a. Do you agree or disagree with the following statement: "Television has too much influence on our lives."
b. Are you optimistic or pessimistic about the future?
c. "Money is ruining sport." What is your reaction to this statement?
d. What will transport be like in the future - especially when supplies of oil run out?

6. Writing about a Book
a. Write an article recommending a book you have read which you particularly enjoyed. Try to say why you think it is such a good book.
b. Write about your favourite character in a book you have read. What kind of person is the character and why is he / she important in the story?

8.8 Speaking – Be Prepared

The next three pages show you how you can prepare for your Speaking exam. This is important because you will do better if you feel prepared, happy, and relaxed. The job of the examiners is to help you to say as much as possible. They are there to encourage you! Read page 192 of this book!

What can I expect?

In this part of the exam you should be ready to do several things:

Talk about yourself
Compare and contrast pictures
Exchange information
Give an opinion on a topic and justify your opinion
Make suggestions
Say what you prefer and why

Despite what some people will tell you, you CAN prepare for this part of the exam. By studying this page you will know what to expect and by studying the next page you will find suggestions for the language you may need.

Personal Information

Here are some typical questions you may be asked. Think about your answers. Can you think of any more questions yourself?

Where do you live / come from?
How long have you lived here / there?
What sort of place is it? What's it like?
What do you like / dislike about it?
What do you do in your free time?
What are your plans for the future?

The Pictures

Look through magazines and newspapers and find pictures about the topics in Section 7 of this book.

Look at two pictures on the same topic and try to speak for one minute, comparing and contrasting the situations you see. Say which one you prefer and why. Which situation looks the more attractive?

Discussion

You and one other candidate will be given some kind of task to discuss with each other. Try to exchange information. The idea is for you both to have a discussion together. Don't try to dominate the discussion. The idea is for you to have the chance to speak and react to each other. This is not a competition. Try to cooperate with the other candidate.

Changing the Subject

If you are asked to talk about a subject you know very little about or aren't really interested in, you might be able to direct the conversation towards something you can talk about. You could say, for example:

.... doesn't really interest me. I prefer ....

or

I'm afraid I don't know very much about ...., but I ....

8.9 **Speaking – Useful Expressions** . . . .

Here are expressions you can use during the Speaking exam. Practise completing them, then say them several times so that they sound natural. Add expressions of your own to the lists.

Giving your opinion
I think that ....
It seems to me that ....
I believe that ....
What I think is that ....

When you're not sure
That's a difficult question.
It's difficult to say.
I'm not really sure, but ....
It's true that ...., but on the other hand ....

Agreeing
Yes, I completely agree.
That's an excellent idea.
Yes, that's what I think too.

Disagreeing
Do you really think so?
That's an interesting idea, but .....
I'm not so sure about that.

Making a suggestion
Why don't we ....
Let's ....
Wouldn't it be better to ....
What about (-ing)
One possibility would be to ....

Likes
I quite like ....
I'm fond of ....
I really love ....

Dislikes
I'm not really very keen on ......
I'm not very fond of ....
I can't stand ....

Saying what you prefer
It's difficult to choose, but I think I prefer ....
I definitely prefer ....
I'd rather ....

Describing a picture
It looks like ....
It seems as if ....
There's a .... at the top / at the bottom / in the middle of the picture.

8.10 Speaking – Possible Topics . . . .

Here are possible topics for discussion with some ideas of language you might use for each. If you are practising in class, try these in pairs or in groups. If you are working alone, try to list as much language related to your topic as possible.

---

1. Recommend suitable holidays in your country to a teenager without much money.

youth hostel   campsite   tent   go hitch-hiking   cheap hotel
bed and breakfast   sleep rough   rucksack   cook for yourself   a cycling holiday

2. What qualities do you look for in an ideal girl / boyfriend or husband / wife?

similar interests   same hobbies   compatible   get on well   good-looking
honest with each other   share same beliefs   sense of humour   intelligent   well-off
it's important that .... it doesn't matter if ....

3. It will soon be your friend's birthday and you want to organise something special for her. Discuss what to do.

a surprise   keep it secret   birthday card   have a party   hire a disco

4. What advice would you give an English-speaking person visiting your country for the first time?

make sure you ......   try to visit ....   don't miss .....   one of the best ....   it's worth -ing

5. A friend of yours has been told by his doctor that he is not fit. What advice would you give him about taking exercise and changing his diet?

buy a bike   go to a gym   work out   start jogging   walk more
avoid alcohol   cut down on ....   eat less ....   eat more ....   between meals

6. You have invited some English-speaking friends to dinner. You want to give them food which is typical of your country. What would you give them?

I'd make ....   We'd start with ....   As a main course   For dessert   We'd drink
It's made with ....   It's got .... in it.   It's a kind of ......   It's like ......   It's a sort of .....

7. There seems to be an increase in violent crime. Think of three things you would do to stop this.

The first thing I'd do would be to ....   I wouldn't allow ....   I'd put a stop to ....
I'd encourage ....   I'm in favour of ....   I'd make it illegal to ....

8. What do you think your life will be like in twenty years time? Try to think of four ways in which life will be better or worse.

There'll be no ......   There'll be much more .....   We won't be -ing

9. Think of the house or flat you live in. Think of ways in which you could improve it - the decoration, the furniture etc.

I'd like to .....   re-paper   re-decorate   get rid of   replace ...... with ....

10. Put these jobs in order of importance:

     doctor   film star   hotel receptionist   road sweeper   shop assistant   teacher
Think of four more and put them in the list. How much salary should each receive per year?

11. Compare and contrast (say what is similar, then say what is different):

a holiday by the sea	vs	a holiday in the country
travelling by car	vs	travelling by train
working in a hotel	vs	working in a department store
watching a video at home	vs	seeing the same film in the cinema
living in a house	vs	living in a flat

Are you organised for the Exam? . . . .

You want to do your best in the exam. It helps if you feel calm, confident, and well-prepared. How can you best prepare before the exam? What should you remember during the exam? Here is advice from an experienced Cambridge examiner.

BEFORE THE EXAM

1. Have you got a supply of pencils and pens to help you write comfortably and legibly?

2. Have you looked again at the right-hand pages of this book - the revision pages?

3. In the Writing Paper you must know how many words you have written. Counting words wastes time. Check how many words you usually write on a line.

4. Have you practised doing two writing tasks within the 90 minute time limit?

5. During the Speaking exam, wear clothes which make you feel good.

6. The evening before the exam, try to do something in English - watch a video, read a book - do something in English for pleasure! What are you going to do?

7. Before the Speaking and Writing exams, revise the vocabulary from Section 7.

8. Have you planned where you will be for the hour before the exam? Make sure you are alone. It might help if you can listen to some of your favourite music. If you are together with your friends, you can make each other nervous. Go somewhere where you can be calm.

DURING THE EXAM

1. Read the instructions for each question carefully and do exactly what they say.

2. Write clearly so that the examiner is able to mark all your work.

3. Remember to read your work 'aloud' in your head - very often you can hear your mistakes.

4. In the multiple choice questions in the first part of Paper 3, look carefully at the words before and after each space. These words can give you a clue.

5. Even if you aren't sure about a multiple-choice question, have a guess!

6. In Paper 3, Question 2, where you have to fill in the blanks, read the whole passage first to get a general understanding of the text. Then look at each sentence.

7. In the Writing exam, read all the subjects very carefully before you choose.

8. In the Writing exam, make a simple plan first, before you start. Then time yourself so that you have an equal amount of time on each question.

9. Remember the mistakes you often make. Take special care to check your work for those particular mistakes.

10. If you find a question too difficult, do your best and move on. Don't worry and don't let it influence the rest of your work!

11. After the exam, don't compare answers with your friends. If you do, and you find you have made a mistake, you panic and start worrying. It is best not to know, and wait for the results!

ANSWER KEY

In some cases there are suggestions for extra vocabulary to add to your lists.

Page 10
1.jealous of 2.full of 3.capable of 4.famous for 5.ashamed of 6.ready for 7.good at 8.responsible for 9.proud of 10.accustomed to 11.typical of 12.aware of 13.dependent on 14.relevant to 15.afraid of

Page 11
1.to 2.of 3.of 4.of 5.of 6.on 7.for 8.of 9.at 10.of 11.of 12.for 13.to 14.for 15.of

Page 12
1.absent from 2.suspicious of 3.sorry for 4.satisfied with 5.late for 6.keen on 7.guilty of 8.opposed to 9.better at 10.short of 11.suitable for 12.similar to 13.terrified of 14.terrible at 15.tired of

Page 13
1.from 2.at 3.of 4.on 5.for 6.to 7.with 8.of 9.to 10.for 11.for 12.of 13.of 14.at 15.of
Extra examples include: acquainted with, amazed at/by, bad/awful/worse at, clever at, eligible for, exempt from, fussy about, fond of, kind to, glad/happy/pleased about, preferable to, quick/slow at, related to, worried about

Page 14
1.resigned from 2.depend on 3.concentrate on 4.insisted on 5.operated on 6.retire from 7.recover from 8.prevent ... from 9.congratulate ... on 10.borrow ... from 11.differs ... from 12.suffer from 13.decided on 14.escape from 15.rely on

Page 15
1.from 2.on 3.on 4.on 5.on 6.from 7.from 8.on 9.on 10.from 11.from 12.on 13.from 14.from 15.from

Page 16
1.consists/ed of 2.remind ... of 3.specialise in 4.succeeded in 5.pay for 6.belongs to 7.objected to 8.search for 9.believed in 10.apologising for 11.blame .. for 12.approve of 13.forgive ... for 14.accused ... of 15.hope for

Page 17
1.of 2.for 3.of 4.in 5.to 6.for 7.of 8.for 9.for 10.to 11.for 12.of 13.for 14.in 15.in
Extra examples include: ask for, choose between, disapprove of, interfere with, listen to, refer to, reply to, smell/taste of, subscribe to, talk about, vote for/against, wait for, worry about

Page 18
1.took ... of 2.paying ... to 3.take ... of 4.took ... of 5.lost ... of 6.keep ... on 7.make ... of 8.Take ... of 9.put ... on 10.caught ... of 11.put ... to 12.pay ... on

Page 19

1.take advantage 2.take care 3.take charge 4.lose count 5.make a fuss 6.take no notice 7.make sense 8.catch sight 9.keep an eye 10.take pity 11.put pressure 12.pay tax 13. play a trick 14.pay attention 15.set fire 16.put a stop (See after Page 21 answers for more expressions.)

Page 20

1.make ... with 2.make ... for 3.take ... for 4.taken ... in 5.took ... in 6.take ... off 7.take ... for 8.make ... for 9.make ... for 10.take ... in 11.made ... with 12.made ... from

Page 21

1.for 2.for 3.for 4.with 5.with 6.from 7.for 8.for 9.for 10.in 11.at 12.off 13.in 14.in 15.in
Extra examples include: declare war on, do business with, find the solution to, give advice about, give a description of, give permission for, have a discussion about, have an effect on, have no objection to, have second thoughts about, lose sight of, make a choice between, make a habit of, make a good impression on, make a mess of, make progress towards, make a reservation for, make a success of, put your trust in, take a decision about, take exception to, take a photograph of

Page 22

Exercise 1 1.f 2.a 3.b 4.d 5.j 6.e 7.g 8.i 9.h 10.c Exercise 2 1.g 2.j 3.f 4.b 5.c 6.a 7.d 8.h 9.e 10.i

Page 23

1.the sun shines 2.a crowd gathers, shouts, boos 3.snow falls 4.a ship sails 5.a plane lands 6.a heart beats, thumps 7.a sweater fits 8.a fire burns 9.a car skids 10.a team loses, plays, trains 11.water boils 12.a dog barks, howls 13.a band plays, marches 14.a colour fades 15.a nose itches

Page 24

Exercise 1 1.f 2.h 3.e 4.i 5.a 6.b 7.c 8.g 9.j 10.d Exercise 2 1.h 2.a 3.c 4.i 5.j 6.d 7.e 8.b 9.f 10.g

Page 25

1.turn a corner, a key 2.hold your breath, a party, a conversation, an interview 3.take place, a seat, a bath, offence, a photograph 4.leave home, a stain 5.give permission, evidence, offence 6.have breakfast, fun, a bath, earache, an operation 7.make a mistake, a speech, a start, a film, a decision 8.catch fire, a fish, a thief 9.do (me) a favour, the washing-up 10.tell the truth, (me) the time 11.change your mind, my clothes, direction 12.keep watch 13.set an example, a trap, standards, a target

Page 26

1.deny 2.missed 3.nodded 4.lowered 5.keep 6.accepted 7.catch 8.hit 9.forgotten 10.lengthen 11.failed 12.hide 13.tightening 14.attacking

Page 27

1.reject 2.defend 3.keep 4.miss 5.deny 6.pass 7.lose 8.borrow 9.enter 10.hit 11.shake 12.lower 13.forget 14.hide 15.lengthen 16.complicate 17.catch 18.loosen 19.save 20.strengthen
Extra examples include: win/lose a game, build/demolish a block of flats, send/receive a letter, capture/release a suspect, deposit/withdraw money, praise/criticise a performance, buy/sell something, obey/break the law, make/lose money

Page 28

1.artificial 2.shallow 3.exact 4.busy 5.calm 6.superior 7.light 8.emotional 9.low 10.flexible 11.stale 12.rapid 13.gentle 14.dark

Page 29

1.natural 2.rough 3.emotional 4.fair 5.shallow 6.approximate 7.rigid 8.poor 9.low 10.heavy 11.severe 12.busy 13.slow 14.smooth 15.considerable 16.fresh 17.mild 18.gentle 19.inferior 20.worthless

Extra examples include: negative/positive attitude, warm/cool welcome, amateur/professional team, ambiguous/clear instructions, permanent/temporary job, major/minor problem, sharp/blunt knife, odd/even number, near/distant future

Page 30

1.in tears 2.in the end 3.in ink 4.in pain 5.in silence 6.In the past 7.in time 8.in public 9.in common 10.in pieces 11.in a moment 12.in love

Page 31

1.common 2.the end 3.error 4.fashion 5.a hurry 6.ink 7.love 8.a moment 9.order 10.pain 11.particular 12.the past 13.pieces 14.public 15.practice 16.silence 17.tears 18.time
Other expressions include: in advance, in charge, in favour (of), in the mood (for), in return, in agreement (with), in a good/bad mood, in other words, in short, in any case, in the long run

Page 32

1.on sale 2.on his own 3.on the phone 4.on time 5.on strike 6.on fire 7.on his mind 8.on foot 9.on guard 10.on the radio 11.on the increase 12.on business

Page 33

1.business 2.credit 3.a diet 4.fire 5.foot 6.guard 7.the increase 8.loan 9.his mind 10.his own 11.the phone 12.purpose 13.the radio 14.sale 15.strike 16.time 17.trial 18.his way
Other expressions include: on behalf of, on the whole, on TV, on duty, on second thoughts, on the contrary, on approval, on display

Page 34

1.out of order 2.out of sight 3.out of tune 4.out of date 5.out of practice 6.out of work 7.out of luck 8.out of control 9.out of doors 10.out of the question 11.out of breath 12.out of reach

Page 35

1.breath 2.control 3.danger 4.date 5.debt 6.doors 7.fashion 8.luck 9.order 10.place 11.practice 12.print 13.the question 14.reach 15.season 16.sight 17.tune 18.work
Other expressions include: out of focus. out of stock, out of hearing, out of character, out of the ordinary

Page 36

by accident, under age, by air, under control, by far, at first, under guarantee, under the impression, for instance, at least, from now on, at present, for sale, at times, without warning
1.under the impression 2.for instance 3.by accident 4.by air 5.At first 6.under age 7.under guarantee 8.for sale 9.without warning 10.at present 11.at least 12.by far 13.at times 14.From now on 15.under control

Page 37

at any rate, by all means, without delay, without doubt, by mistake, under pressure, from time to time, for the time being

Other expressions include: at a glance, at last, at the latest, at war (with), at once, at sea, at work, at short notice, at a disadvantage, at risk, at a profit/loss

by heart, by chance, by the way, by no means, by name, by sight

for a while, for now/the moment, for ages, for ever, for a change

from bad to worse, from then on, from personal experience, from what I can gather

under no obligation, under suspicion, under her thumb, under an assumed name, under his influence, under discussion

without fail, without exception, without my parents' consent, without success, without a break

Page 38

1.far 2.objected 3.on 4.of 5.ready/prepared/dressed 6.for 7.missed 8.make 9.on 10.late 11.turned/reached 12.look 13.in 14.breath 15.dog 16.pay 17.beating 18.at 19.aware 20.in

Page 40

Exercise 1 1.blow up 2.beat ... up 3.gone up 4.turn up 5.speak up 6.brush up 7.call ... up 8.clear up Exercise 2 1.get up 2.dress up 3.back ... up 4.stay up 5.came up 6.catching up 7.sum up 8.mixing ... up

Page 41

1.back 2.beat 3.blow 4.brush 5.call 6.catch 7.clear 8.come 9.dress 10.get 11.go 12.mix 13.speak 14.stay 15.sum 16.turn

Page 42

Exercise 1 1.eats/has eaten up 2.owned up 3.lit up 4.shot up 5.build up 6.grow up 7.added up 8.bundled up Exercise 2 1.look ... up 2.brighten up 3.cheer ... up 4.piled up 5.drew up 6.hung up 7.brought up 8.turn ... up

Page 43

Exercise 1 1.d 2.b 3.c 4.f 5.e 6.h 7.a 8.g Exercise 2 1.d 2.b 3.a 4.e 5.g 6.c 7.f 8.h

Page 44

Exercise 1 1.pick ... up 2.held up 3.put up 4.make up 5.do up 6.give up 7.take ... up 8.set up Exercise 2 1.held up 2.took up 3.made up 4.done ... up 5.put ... up 6.gave up 7.picked up 8.set up

Page 45

1.set up 2.pick up 3.do up 4.make up 5.take up 6.give up 7.hold up 8.put up

Other verbs include: book up, lock up, pack up, think up, use up, cut up, heat up, tune up, pay up, clean up

Page 46

Exercise 1 1.let ... down 2.died down 3.mark ... down 4.Slow down 5.jot down 6.live ... down 7.cut down 8.play down Exercise 2 1.run down 2.laid down 3.shouted down 4.backed down 5.getting ... down 6.settle down 7.poured down 8.closed down

Page 47

1.back 2.close 3.cut 4.die 5.get 6.jot 7.lay 8.let 9.live 10.mark 11.play 12.pour 13.run 14.settle 15.shout 16.slow

Page 48

Exercise 1 1.knocked down 2.put down 3.bring down 4.come down 5.turn down 6.broke down 7.gone down 8.took down Exercise 2 1.Turn ... down 2.put down 3.taken down 4.bring down 5.broke down 6.knock ... down 7.gone down 8.came down

Page 49

1.knock down 2.turn down 3.bring down 4.put down 5.take down 6.come down 7.go down 8.break down

Other verbs include: hold down, keep down, stand down, lay down, track down, burn down, cool down

Page 50

Exercise 1 1.backed out 2.pointed out 3.broke out 4.eat out 5.sort ... out 6.burnt/burned out 7.stand out 8.left ... out Exercise 2 1.get out 2.ran out 3.passed out 4.find out 5.wear ... out 6.shot out 7.hand out 8.Look out

Page 51

1.back 2.burn 3.break 4.eat 5.find 6.get 7.hand 8.leave 9.look 10.pass 11.point 12.run 13.shoot 14.sort 15.stand 16.wear

Page 52

Exercise 1 1.pulled out 2.walked out 3.died out 4.break out 5.brought out 6.fall out 7.running out 8.rule out Exercise 2 1.work out 2.carry out 3.cross out 4.wash out 5.burst out 6.sit ... out 7.check out 8.drop out

Page 53

Exercise 1 1.h 2.f 3.d 4.a 5.e 6.b 7.g 8.c Exercise 2 1.h 2.b 3.e 4.f 5.g 6.c 7.d 8.a

Page 54

Exercise 1 1.taking ... out 2.come out 3.make out 4.let out 5.put ... out 6.went out 7.turned out 8.set out Exercise 2 1.takes out 2.made out 3.come out 4.put out 5.let out 6.turned out 7.set out 8.goes/went out

Page 55

1.put out 2.let out 3.set out 4.take out 5.turn out 6.make out 7.come out 8.go out
Other verbs include: speak out, throw out, hand out, catch out, cut out, ask someone out, read something out, cry out

Page 56

Exercise 1 1.pull off 2.slip off 3.put off 4.stop off 5.show off 6.let ... off 7.see ... off 8.write off Exercise 2 1.putting ... off 2.drop ... off 3.telling ... off 4.cut ... off 5.getting off 6.went off 7.set ... off 8.kicked off

Page 57

1.cut 2.drop 3.get 4.go 5.kick 6.let 7.pull 8.put 9.see 10.set 11.show 12.slip 13.stop 14.tell 15.write

Page 58

Exercise 1 1.dropped off 2.called off 3.went off 4.keep off 5.take off 6.wear off 7.turn off 8.shake ... off Exercise 2 1.takes off 2.ring off 3.pay off 4.fall off 5.holds off 6.gave off 7.lay off 8.set off

Page 59

Exercise 1 1.g 2.d 3.h 4.f 5.c 6.b 7.a 8.e Exercise 2 1.d 2.e 3.g 4.f 5.c 6.b 7.a 8.h
Other verbs include: come off, break off, fence off

Page 60

Exercise 1 1.carried on 2.pick on 3.send on 4.stay on 5.cheered ... on 6.set ... on 7.hold on 8.catch on Exercise 2 1.switched ... on 2.try ... on 3.count on 4.live on 5.touched on 6.move on 7.looked on 8.drag on

Page 61

1.carry 2.catch 3.cheer 4.count 5.drag 6.hold 7.live 8.look 9.move 10.pick 11.send 12.set 13.stay 14.switch 15.touch 16.try

Page 62

Exercise 1 1.getting on 2.keep ... on 3.put on 4.Come on 5.turn ... on 6.go on 7.calling on 8.take on Exercise 2 1.go on 2.keep on 3.put on 4.take on 5.coming on 6.call on 7.get on 8.turned on

Page 63

1.get on 2.put on 3.turn on 4.take on 5.keep on 6.call on 7.go on 8.come on
Other verbs include: hang on, jump on, pass on, let on

Page 64

Exercise 1 1.hand in 2.flooded in 3.show in 4.check in 5.sink in 6.step in 7.join in 8.stopping in
Exercise 2 1.burst into 2.pulled into 3.bumped into 4.looking into 5.turned ... into 6.talk ... into 7.go into 8.rush into

Page 65

1.check 2.flood 3.hand 4.join 5.show 6.sink 7.step 8.stop 9.bump 10.burst 11.go 12.look 13.pull 14.rush 15.talk 16.turn

Page 66

Exercise 1 1.call in 2.put in 3.taken in 4.bring in 5.came in 6.gets in 7.broke in 8.fill in
Exercise 2 1.filling in 2.break in 3.get in 4.take in 5.brought in 6.call in 7.put in 8.coming in

Page 67

1.break in 2.fill in 3.put in 4.get in 5.take in 6.call in 7.bring in 8.come in
Other verbs include: get into, run into, trick someone into -ing, fit in, pop in, drop in, give in, turn in

Page 68

Exercise 1 1.go with 2.taken over 3.comes to 4.get round 5.saw through 6.put through 7.pressing for 8.turned away Exercise 2 1.get by 2.heard from 3.takes after 4.see to 5.bring ... round 6.pull through 7.came across 8.get away

Page 69

1.bring round 2.come across 3.come to 4.get away 5.get by 6.get round 7.go with 8.hear from 9.push for 10.pull through 11.put through 12.see through 13.see to 14.take after 15.take over 16.turn away

Page 70

Exercise 1 1.fishing for 2.put by 3.ran over 4.stick to 5.toying with 6.pay back 7.leap at 8.brushed aside Exercise 2 1.run through 2.stand for 3.get at 4.take back 5.falling for 6.attend to 7.cut back 8.brings back

Page 71

Exercise 1 1.a 2.g 3.d 4.e 5.b 6.f 7.h 8.c Exercise 2 1.b 2.d 3.g 4.a 5.h 6.e 7.c 8.f

Page 72

Exercise 1 1.get over 2.call for 3.put forward 4.come round 5.stand by 6.go through 7.come over 8.gave away Exercise 2 1.put forward 2.standing by 3.get ... over 4.come over 5.given away 6.go through 7.calling for 8.come round

Page 73

1.give away 2.stand by 3.call for 4.come over 5.get over 6.put forward 7.come round 8.go through

Page 74

back out of, carry on with, catch up on, catch up with, cut down on, drop out of, fit in with, look back on, run out of, stand in for 1.drop out of 2.back out of 3.caught up with 4.cutting down on 5.fit in with 6.catch up on 7.look back on 8.stand in for 9.carry on with 10.run out of

Page 75

1.out of 2.on with 3.up with 4.up on 5.down on 6.out of 7.in with 8.back on 9.out of 10.in for

Page 76

1.in for 2.up with 3.away with 4.up to 5.up to 6.back on 7.up to 8.round to 9.down with 10.back on 11.in for 12.through with

Page 77

1.come in for 2.come up with 3.do away with 4.face up to 5.feel up to 6.fall back on 7.get up to 8.get round to 9.go down with 10.go back on 11.go in for 12.go through with

Page 78

1.out of 2.up with 3.in on 4.up to 5.up to 6.down on 7.forward to 8.up for 9.up with 10.up for 11.up to 12.out on

Page 79

1.out of 2.up with 3.in on 4.up to 5.down on 6.forward to 7.up to 8.up for 9.up with 10.up for 11.up to 12.out on

Page 80

1.gave up smoking 2.put off the meeting/put the meeting off 3.run out of 4.time to get over 5.they turn up 6.put you up 7.stand in for Brian 8.get round to answering 9.put up with 10.looks down on 11.fall back on 12.had backed me up

Page 82

(in)attentive, (un)attractive, (un)comfortable, (in)competent, (in)formal, (un)healthy, (in)offensive, (un)predictable, (un)reasonable, (un)reliable 1.unreliable 2.uncomfortable 3.informal 4.incompetent 5.unreasonable 6.unattractive 7.inattentive 8.unhealthy 9.unpredictable 10.inoffensive

Page 83

decide/decision, indecisive excuse, inexcusable expense, inexpensive sense, insensitive consider, inconsiderate believe/belief, unbelievable fortune, unfortunate help, unhelpful profit, unprofitable succeed/success, unsuccessful
Other examples: depend,independent effect,ineffective offend,inoffensive condition,unconditional employ,unemployed favour,unfavourable law,unlawful luck,unlucky please,unpleasant

Page 84

(non-)alcoholic, harmful/less, (dis)honest, (il)logical, (dis)obedient, (dis)organised, painful/less, (im)patient, tactful/less, (non-)violent 1.harmless 2.dishonest 3.painless 4.disorganised 5.non-violent 6.tactless 7.non-alcoholic 8.disobedient 9.illogical 10.impatient

Page 85

agree, disagreeable loyalty, disloyal reputation, disreputable satisfy/satisfaction, dissatisfied care, careful/less think/thought, thoughtful/less use, useful/less illegal illegible immature improbable exist/existence, non-existent
Other examples: approve,disapproving connect,disconnected fruitful/less literacy,illiterate immobile imperfect impossible impractical non-essential, non-stop

Page 86

1.incredibly 2.heavily 3.possibly 4.dramatically 5.shyly 6.noisily 7.unavoidably 8.Naturally 9.sarcastically 10.legibly 11.Unfortunately 12.comparatively 13.Basically 14.reliably 15.shabbily

Page 88

disappear, disapprove, misbehave, misinform, enlarge, unload, unlock, misjudge, ensure, misunderstand, unwrap 1.misinformed 2.enlarging 3.unlocked 4.misbehave 5.disapproves/ed 6.disappeared 7.unloaded 8.misunderstand 9.disobeying 10.unwrapped 11.misjudged 12.ensure

Page 89

disable, disconnect, discourage, discredit, disqualify, distrust misinterpret, mislead, mistrust enable, encourage, entrust unpack, unscrew
Other examples: disarm, disorganise/ize, displease, disprove miscalculate, mismanage, misread, misplace, mislay endanger, enrage unbutton, uncover, undress, unplug, unwind

Other examples with prefixes include: decentralise/ize, devalue; reappear, rearrange, recapture, reconstruct, recycle, renew, repay, reunite; overcharge, overestimate, overload, overrule; undercharge, underestimate

Page 90
1.blood 2.anxious 3.disbelief 4.confirmation 5.advice 6.cooperation 7.disapproving 8.conclusion 9.contribution 10.assistant 11.contradictory 12.uncommunicative 13.choice 14.analytical

Page 91
1.advise, advice 2.analytical, analyst, analysis 3.anxiety 4.(dis)approving, (dis)approval 5.assistant 6.(un)believable, (dis)belief 7.bloody, blood 8.choose, choice 9.(un)communicative, communication 10.(in)conclusive, conclusion 11.(un)confirmed, confirmation 12.contradictory, contradiction 13.contributory, contributor contribution 14.(un)cooperative, cooperation

Page 92
1.criticise/ize 2.deepened 3.destructive 4.insistent 5.failing 6.inclusive 7.integrated 8.instructors 9.growth 10.heights 11.flight 12.deafening 13.demonstators 14.undeniable

Page 93
1.(un)critical, criticism 2.deafen, deafening 3.(un)demonstrative, demonstrator, demonstration 4.(un)deniable, denial 5.deepen, deep 6.destroy, destructive 7.failing, failure 8.fly, flying, flight 9.grow, growth 10.heighten 11.include, inclusive 12.insistent, insistence 13.integrated, integration 14.instructive, instructor, instruction

Page 94
1.unpleasant 2.length 3.unpredictable 4.relief 5.unreliable 6.strenghtened 7.shortage 8.suitable 9.surviving 10.widen 11.refusal 12.optimism 13.performance 14.pessimistic

Page 95
1.lengthen, long 2.optimistic, optimism 3.perform, performance 4.pessimistic, pessimist 5.(un)pleasant, (dis)pleasure 6.(un)predictable, prediction 7.refusal 8.relieve, relief 9.rely, (un)reliable 10.shorten, shortage 11.strengthen, strong 12.suit, (un)suitable 13.surviving, survivor 14.widen, wide.

Page 96
1.definitions 2.indefinite 3.economise/ize 4.economists 5.identical 6.identification 7.illustration 8.imaginative 9.impressed 10.impressionable 11.live 12.living 13.proposed 14.reality 15.various 16.varied

Page 97
1.define, (in)definite, definition 2.economise/ize, (un)economic, economist, economy 3.identify, (un)identified, identical, identification 4.illustrated, illustrator, illustration 5.imaginary, imagination 6.impressionable, (un)impressive 7.lively, alive, life 8.proposed, proposal 9.(un)realistic, reality 10.vary, various, varied, (in)variable, variety

Page 98
1.anxious 2.confirmation 3.impressed 4.reputable 5.insistent 6.optimistically 7.definitely 8.Unfortunately 9.flight 10.displeasure 11.patience 12.unsuccessful 13.choice 14.noisy 15.relief 16.Naturally 17.unrealistic 18.disappeared 19.useless 20.strength

Page 100

Exercise 1 1.apologise 2.regret 3.excuse 4.sorry 5.forgive 6.apologetic 7.apology

Exercise 2 1.persuade 2.advice 3.advise 4.insist 5.make 6.suggest Exercise 3 1.However 2.though 3.Despite 4.Although 5.in spite

Page 101

Possible sentences: 1.Although he was rich, he wasn't happy., Despite all his money, he wasn't happy. 2.She gave me some advice about what to do., She advised me what to do. 3.Bring that over **here**., Take that over **there**. 4.She left a note on the table to say where she had gone., On the wall there was a notice saying smoking was forbidden. 5.I borrowed some money from my friend., My friend lent me some money. 6.They will probably raise some of their prices., Some prices will probably rise.

Page 102

Exercise 1 1.aware 2.sensible 3.apparent 4.familiar 5.accustomed 6.sensitive 7.sense Exercise 2 1.the same 2.shared 3.similar 4.like 5.common 6.alike 7.identical Exercise 3 1.rejected 2.refused 3.denied 4.disagreed 5.disapproved 6.objected

Page 103

Possible sentences: 1.She's a sensible person so she'll know what to do., She's very sensitive to criticism 2.Her dress is identical **to** mine., Her dress is the same **as** mine. 3.He had worked very hard so he was tired., He had done hardly any work so he wasn't tired. 4.If the sweater doesn't fit, you can try another size., I'm afraid grey doesn't really suit you. 5.Would it be convenient for you to see me tomorrow afternoon?, We haven't found anyone who's really suitable for the job. 6.He happened to mention the letter during our conversation., I expected him to refer **to** the letter during our conversation.

Page 104

Exercise 1 1.Only 2.except 3.beside 4.Apart 5.besides 6.Instead 7.otherwise Exercise 2 1.protect 2.prevent 3.guard 4.divert 5.avoid Exercise 3 1.successful 2.fit 3.possible 4.succeed 5.capable 6.manage 7.skilled

Page 105

Possible sentences: 1.I was able to avoid seeing her again., I was able to prevent **him from** seeing her again. 2.Did you manage **to do** it?, Did you succeed **in doing** it? 3.We have to check every suitcase in case someone is carrying a bomb., You use these levers to control the machine. 4.The centre had to close down due to a lack of funds., The attempt to break the record ended in failure. 5.They'll dismiss him if he keeps coming to work late., Don't resign before you're sure you've got another job to go to. 6.I must remember to phone my mother., I must remind her to phone her mother.

Page 106

Exercise 1 1.keen 2.fascinated 3.interested 4.appeal 5.fond 6.fancy 7.glad

Exercise 2 1.condemned 2.complained 3.accused 4.charged 5.blamed 6.arrested 7.sentenced 8.protested Exercise 3 1.permit 2.permission 3.let 4.allow 5.agree

Page 107

Possible sentences: 1.I suppose I'm quite fond **of** her., I'm not very keen **on** working late tonight. 2.Why did he allow them **to leave?,** Why did he let them **leave?** 3.They will announce the decision to the press., They will inform the press of their decision. 4.They won first prize in the competition., There's a reward of 100 dollars if you find the missing necklace. 5.I think we're going in the wrong direction., We asked for directions to the police station. 6.Could you tell me the way to the town hall?, They walked along the path through the woods.

Page 108

1.C 2.A 3.D 4.B 5.A 6.D 7.D 8.C 9.D 10.C 11.B 12.B 13.C 14.B 15.A 16.B

Page 110

Exercise 1 1. b.better than c.as well as 2. a.a more careful driver than c.as carefully as
Exercise 2 1.has a warmer climate than 2.eat as fast as 3.the most powerful drill 4.nobody works as hard 5.strangest person I've ever 6.wasn't as interesting as 7.the best badminton player

Page 112

Exercise 1 1.so 2.so 3.So 4.such a 5.such 6.such Exercise 2 1.was so small 2.so much noise 3.such strong coffee that we 4.writes so badly 5.had/'d never seen such a 6.drove so slowly 7.so little time that we

Page 113

1.so cold 2.so quietly 3.so much money 4.such a shame 5.such high prices 6.such loud music

1.**so** violent, cheap, angry, dark 2.**so** quickly, carelessly, deeply, dangerously 3.**so** much time, few ideas, little time, many people 4.**such a** loud bang, an historic city, a warm bed, a difficult question 5.**such** clothes, awful children, terrible storms, high mountains 6.**such** lovely weather, fresh bread, heavy rain, pleasant music

Page 114

1.avoid staying out 2.great difficulty (in) understanding 3.prevented me from speaking 4.apologised for being 5.accused Sophie of breaking her 6.keen on playing 7.use shouting 8.instead of playing 9.objects to getting up 10.you mind not repeating 11.prefers watching TV 12.used to driving

Page 115

Possible examples:

Preposition + -ing: instead of looking miserable, without paying, after leaving school, by working hard

Adjective + preposition + -ing: keen on playing football, used/accustomed to driving this car, interested in being an engineer, good at making excuses, worried about meeting her parents, capable of understanding

Verb + -ing: avoid meeting her, give up/stop smoking, mind (not) repeating that, prefer staying in to going out, keep making mistakes

Verb + preposition + ing: prevent me from leaving, accuse her of stealing it, object to paying extra, look forward to seeing you, congratulate her on coming first, thank them for coming

Page 116

1.old enough 2.advised Kate to wear 3.would/'d prefer you to 4.difficult for older people to 5.is/'s said to be living 6.have let them leave 7.was too complicated for me 8.I would/'d rather not talk 9.persuade Murray to sing them 10.you happen to know 11.seem to have left 12.had/'d better not see

Page 117

Possible examples:

Verb + infinitive: happen to know, promise to come, hope to see you, hesitate to criticise, arrange to meet him, try/attempt to understand

Verb + [icon] + infinitive: advise her to leave, would prefer you to come back later, persuade him to contribute, forbid him to see her, encourage them to try again, remind her to be on time; hear him come in, watch her open her present, let them escape, make him work harder

Page 118

Exercise 1 1.have/'ve been trying 2.have/'ve never driven 3.has/'s stolen 4.have/'ve visited 5.have/'ve been standing 6.have/'ve eaten Exercise 2 1.has/'s been working here for 2.first time I have/'ve had 3.has not/hasn't seen him since 4.have/'ve been to Athens three 5.happier than I've ever 6.has not/hasn't been tidied 7.have not/haven't eaten (anything) for

Page 120

1.asked Stuart if he was 2.refused to eat her 3.the train had never been 4.begged them to let her 5.asked where the meeting was 6.'d better take your 7.said she was having her 8.John not to make 9.to know what they were 10.offered to come if she 11.wondered why they had/'d looked 12.that he look for/that he looked for/that he should look for

Page 122

Exercise 1 1.apologises 2.had/'d known 3.improves 4.would have arrived 5.would/'d take 6.had/'d gone Exercise 2 1.had/'d had enough money 2.unless you revise 3.me, I'd never have 4.hadn't been driving so 5.went to bed earlier 6.if he does not/doesn't arrive 7.wish I had not/hadn't eaten

Page 124

Exercise 1 1.is made 2.was made 3.is being made 4.had been made 5.has been made 6.will be made Exercise 2 1.are closed 2.has not/hasn't been cleaned 3.is/'s being interviewed 4.had just been bought by 5.decision will be made by 6.must have been seen by 7.must be taken

Page 126

1.me why I hadn't 2.play as well as 3.believed to have travelled 4.such a bad driver 5.objected to Sarah watching him 6.I would/'d rather come 7.only I had/'d asked 8.decision was made by 9.wondered which room it was 10.strongest man I've ever 11.too stale 12.used to writing

Page 128

1.Top tennis players don't smoke. 2.I live in Belmont Road. 3.The team didn't play as well as I had expected. 4.The news is so depressing at the moment. 5.They asked him where the police station was. 6.Is he coming too?—I hope not. 7.I don't have enough money. 8.Go along Cromwell Street. 9.Have you got a room of your own?/Have you got your own room? 10.We had such a good time. 11.In my country we start school when we are six. 12.They have four children who are very amusing.

Page 130

1.I have been living here in Spain for 2 years. 2.I have/'ve lived/been living here since I was 10 years old. 3.She was born in 1900. 4.I try my best not to make mistakes. 5.We have had such terrible weather. 6.She always went to work by bus. 7.I can't see you until the day after tomorrow. 8.We didn't have to go to school 9.I have/'ve never been there before. 10.Are you interested in learning this or not? 11.My sister is twenty years old./My sister is twenty. 12.When you come tomorrow, can you bring the book I lent you?

Page 138

1.main course 2.low-calorie spread 3.breakfast cereal 4.list of ingredients 5.taste 6.vegetarian 7.peel the potatoes 8.beat the eggs 9.local market 10.fast food 11.empty, add, stir, boil, simmer 12.speciality 13.dressing 14.slice of toast 15.additives 16.spices

Page 139

1.cut 2.chop 3.grate 4.pour 5.beat 6.divide 7.melt 8.bake 9.sprinkle 10.serve

Page 140

1.on a diet 2.upset easily 3.parting 4.look my best 5.impulsive 6.bald patch 7.shy 8.courage 9.speak openly 10.curly hair 11.extrovert 12.piercing eyes 13.very proud 14.have the sense 15.spiteful 16.lose my temper

Page 141

Positive/negative etc.: This is a matter of opinion, so there is no correct answer!

Page 142

1.sponsor 2.train really hard 3.first round 4.explain the rules 5.keen on 6.play cards 7.disqualified 8.take part in 9.cheer 10.member 11.tactical game 12.draw 13.championship 14.lack of support 15.final score 16.take up

Page 144

1.break in 2.forged money 3.community service 4.on probation 5.vandalised 6.witness 7.shoplifting 8.fined 9.plead guilty 10.admit 11.reach a verdict 12.smuggling drugs 13.prove 14.arrest 15.death penalty 16.terrorist

Page 145

Crimes: arson—starting a fire illegally, assault—attacking violently, blackmail—getting payment for not revealing secrets, burglary—stealing from a house at night, kidnapping—stealing a person (to get money for their return), selling drugs—selling illegal substances which act as stimulants, shoplifting—stealing from shops, smuggling watches—taking watches into a country illegally, vandalism—destroying property
Other crimes include: robbery—stealing from a person or place, mugging—assault and robbery, forgery—making an illegal copy of a banknote, painting, signatures etc, rape—forcing someone to have sex, hi-jacking—getting control of a plane etc. to steal from it, or to force people to do something, fraud—getting money by tricking people

Page 146

1.converted 2.double glazing 3.lounge 4.gadget 5.installed 6.replace the fuse 7.doing the washing-up 8.wardrobe 9.terraced 10.spare bedroom 11.lay the table 12.household chores 13.storage space 14.landing 15.share a flat 16.cellar

Page 148

1.fully insured 2.holiday resort 3.twin-bedded room 4.make friends 5.package holiday 6.get a tan 7.guest house 8.sightseeing tour 9.entertainment facilities 10.glossy brochure 11.put on a show 12.self-catering 13.tourist information office 14.change money 15.activity holiday 16.deposit

Page 150

1.subtitled 2.special effects 3.clapped 4.series 5.final scene 6.commercials 7.rehearse 8.cartoon characters 9.another channel 10.stunt 11.perform live 12.directed 13.stars 14.choir 15.reviews 16.hit

Page 152

1.enrol for 2.fees 3.specialise in 4.diploma 5.school uniform 6.cheat 7.maintain discipline 8.boarding school 9.co-educational 10.course work 11.under great pressure 12.sandwich course 13.secondary school 14.revise for 15.brush up 16.relevant to

Page 153

Possible subjects: English, mathematics/maths, science (physics, chemistry, biology,), technology, computer science, information technology (word processing etc), woodwork, metalwork, history, geography, economics, art, handicraft, music, gymnastics, games, home economics, cookery

Page 154

1.rush hour 2.traffic jams 3.exhaust fumes 4.polluting 5.public transport 6.subsidised fares 7.switch to 8.quality of life 9.pesticides 10.food chain 11.dramatic increase 12.research 13.cut down on 14.nuclear waste 15.alternative sources

Page 156

1.blocks of flats 2.housing estate 3.pedestrian precinct 4.building site 5.multi-storey car park 6.wander 7.quiet suburb 8.make way for 9.outskirts 10.rural life 11.litter 12.main crops 13.hedge 14.spoil the view 15.tiny cottage 16.property prices

Page 158

1.speed limit 2.on board 3.luggage rack 4.itinerary 5.cut-price fares 6.get a lift 7.serviced 8.reclining seats 9.more economical 10.bumpy flight 11.commute 12.skidded 13.unavoidably delayed 14.change trains 15.economy class 16.collided with

Page 160

1.responsibility 2.promoted 3.retire 4.permanent post 5.resign 6.commission 7.work overtime 8.fire 9.assembly line 10.night shift 11.ambitious 12.good impression 13.fringe benefit 14.deal with 15.job satisfaction 16.manual work

Page 162

1.held 2.commemorate 3.lasts 4.dress up 5.opening ceremony 6.colourful procession 7.floats 8.sponsored 9.street entertainers 10.erected 11.stalls 12.traditional crafts 13.puppet shows 14.attracts 15.local event 16.tourist attraction

Page 164

1.bargain 2.out of stock 3.local shops 4.try it on 5.can't afford 6.take it back 7.rate of exchange 8.go with 9.loan 10.faulty goods 11.street market 12.window shopping 13.insurance company 14.get a discount 15.refund 16.on credit

Page 166

1.keep fit 2.recover from 3.visiting hours 4.injured 5.upset stomach 6.private patient 7.relieve the pain 8.health service 9.outbreak 10.spread 11.highly infectious 12.successfully treated 13.operate on 14.come out in 15.stress-related 16.regular exercise

Page 167

1.e 2.d 3.f 4.h 5.b 6.g 7.a 8.c

Page 168

1.computer networks 2.major breakthrough 3.labour-saving devices 4.locate resources 5.mass-produced 6.come to terms with 7.database 8.strict safeguards 9.repetitive tasks 10.made redundant 11.monitor 12.safety features 13.under development 14.genetic engineering 15.life expectancy 16.taken for granted

Page 170

1.civil ceremony 2.gets on my nerves 3.break the ice 4.acquaintance 5.backgrounds 6.divorce rate 7.split up 8.house on fire 9.make friends 10.good company 11.in common 12.foster homes 13.for the sake of 14.on speaking terms 15.date 16.happily married

Page 171

Positive: 2, 4, 7, 8, 13, 14 Negative: 1, 3, 5, 6, 9, 10, 11, 12, 15, 16

Page 172

1.increase circulation 2.press conference 3.current affairs 4.pick up 5.speculation 6.special issue 7.cable television 8.news flash 9.live coverage 10.editorial 11.unbiased account 12.obituary 13.headline 14.respect for privacy 15.spokesperson 16.in depth

Page 174

1.mild climate 2.gust of wind 3.changeable 4.pouring down 5.global warming 6.widespread damage 7.cut off 8.struck by lightning 9.sticky 10.hot spell 11.dark clouds 12.turned out 13.we're in for 14.bitterly cold 15.heavy rain 16.weather forecast

Page 178

Exercise 1 1.When they fly to Switzerland they always take a Swissair flight from London. 2.At Christmas they stayed at a French hotel and at New Year they stayed at a Scottish hotel. 3.The Grand Hotel is famous for its restaurant. 4.Princess Diana is Queen Elizabeth's daughter-in-law. 5.My favourite horror film is 'Bride of Frankenstein'. 6.He was born on a Wednesday morning in the middle of February. 7.The capital of the United States is Washington. 8.Last summer I went to Germany to learn German at a language school.
Exercise 2 As it was January and the middle of summer, the sun was beating down as the passengers got on the plane. Some time after it had taken off, the pilot made an announcement: "This is Captain Davis speaking. If there is a doctor on board, could he or she inform a member of the cabin staff?" When she heard this, Maria called a steward, who took her to the back of the plane. There she found a German passenger, who was obviously in great pain. It was clear that he was suffering from appendicitis and needed to go to a hospital. The

captain decided to divert the plane to Darwin. From the airport the passenger was taken by ambulance to the nearest hospital, where surgeons successfully removed his appendix.

Page 180
Exercise 1 1.until 2.before 3.Although 4.as if 5.because 6.so that 7.if 8.While 9.who 10.When 11.that 12.which 13.Unfortunately 14.but 15.so 16.Just as

Page 181
Exercise 2 1.just as 2.as soon as 3.by the time 4.as long as 5.unless 6.even though 7.where 8. in case Exercise 3 1.Luckily 2.Naturally 3.Meanwhile 4.Eventually 5.Because of this 6.Despite this 7.On the other hand 8.Some time later

Page 182
1.Thanks 2.I'm sorry 3.really busy 4.Congratulations 5.of course 6.As you know 7.in the end 8.get on 9.Anyway 10.put you up 11.let me know 12.Best wishes

Page 184
1.With reference to 2.current issue 3.send me information 4.particularly interested 5.package holidays 6.under what circumstances 7.eligible for 8.mentioned 9.However 10.grateful 11.additional charge 12.look forward to

Лицензия № 070011 от 17.06.96. Подписано в печать 15.01.97. Формат 62 × 84/8. Печать офсетная.
Бумага офсетная № 1. Усл. печ. л. 24,27. Усл. кр.-отт. 25,2. Тираж 5000 экз. Зак. № 1215.
Издательство «Титул». 249020 г. Обнинск Калужской обл., ул. Курчатова, 21, а/я 5055.
Отпечатано с оригинал-макета в ОАО «Можайский полиграфический комбинат».
143200 г. Можайск Московской обл., ул. Мира, 93.